Cellarmanship

Patrick O'Neill

CAMRA BOOKS

Published by Campaign for Real Ale
230 Hatfield Road
St Albans
Hertfordshire AL1 4LW

www.camra.org.uk

First published 1981
Second edition 1992
Reprinted 1994
Third edition 1997
Fourth edition 2005

ISBN 1 85249 208 2

*A CIP catalogue record for this book is
available from the British Library.*

Printed and bound in the UK by
William Clowes Limited, Beccles, Suffolk

Commissioning Editor: Joanna Copestick
Copy Editor: Jill Adams
Designer: Dale Tomlinson
Illustrations: Patrick O'Neill
Publications Coordinator: Cressida Feiler

Words that appear in **bold** are defined in the *Glossary* on page 127.

Contents

Illustrations

Preface to the fourth edition

'The cellarman belongs to the earthworm class.
He has his habitat underground, and only emerges at
intervals to receive cellar goods as they are delivered
by the drayman, or to take up supplies to the bars ...
Strength is a prerequisite for a cellarman –
the weakling has no place in a cellar.'
LICENSED HOUSES AND THEIR MANAGEMENT, 1950

This book has been a quarter of a century in the making. The first edition, started in 1980, published in 1981, was a slender volume printed straight from my typewritten pages. Nevertheless, it was well received and in 1992 CAMRA published my revised and much enlarged second edition, which was reprinted in 1994. In 1997 a third edition, again revised and with more added material, was produced by the late Ivor Clissold, a friend and colleague, missed by all who knew him. This then is the fourth edition, again revised to include new developments and reflect modern practices.

During the past 25 years the pub and brewing industry has seen more change than in the preceding century. One consistent trend has been the attempts, frequently misguided, by brewers to de-skill the art of looking after beer. Fortunately many of these initiatives that were setting off in false directions have come to nothing and there is now a general realisation that cask-conditioned beer (real ale) is a quality, craft-made product and is truly worthy of care and attention in its keeping. CAMRA has done much to foster and justify this climate. This book continues to demonstrate our duty of care for real ale.

PATRICK O'NEILL

Author's Acknowledgements

The opinions contained in this work are entirely the author's. Statements do not represent the views of any particular section of the Licensed Trade and do not necessarily reflect all aspects of the policies of the Campaign for Real Ale (CAMRA).

Grateful acknowledgements are extended to many, many CAMRA members, cellar fitters, brewers, publicans and others who have provided hours of discussion and advice over a quarter century of interest in these topics.

The diagrams, which were all drawn anew for this edition, are also solely the work of the author and, except where specifically mentioned, are not intended to represent any particular manufacturer's equipment.

Introduction

THIS BOOK IS intended to be a textbook. Its aim is neither to imbue cask-conditioned beer, real ale, with any rosy glow of nostalgia nor to put forward any polemical position. It simply recognises that caring for cask-conditioned beer, a product now almost unique to Great Britain, requires some learnt skills and techniques. However it also tries to go quite a lot further in providing the scientific reasoning backing these techniques. Although fully understanding these elements of physics and chemistry may not be strictly necessary to be a good cellarman, such comprehension will add greatly to job satisfaction and lead to increased confidence.

At this point it should be said that in this work the words **cellarman** and **cellarmanship** are used throughout without any implication of gender specificity but purely to avoid textual clumsiness. It must be understood that the opinions contained in the text are entirely the author's and do not necessarily reflect any specific CAMRA viewpoint. The numerous references to technical measurements involve many engineering, scientific and practical units. In general, rather than translating everything into metric units, those most commonly used in the pub/brewing trade are used with equivalents given where appropriate. For beer volumes at the customer level the Imperial pint is sacrosanct.

Brewing, as with other centuries-old, craft-based trades, has developed its own set of special terms – almost a secret language – for often quite simple and mundane things. Many of these terms will be used in this book and whenever they first appear will be emphasised in **bold** type. Although using these terms may seem to some an affectation, it does lead to precise understanding and can avoid some real confusion. Most terms are also listed in the Glossary, Appendix 5.

The worst instance of this is the simple word **barrel**. Throughout the pub trade this little word is under constant abuse – 'I'm just going down to change the barrel...', 'We sold four barrels of that last week!' – examples are endless. If this book could only do one thing, then correcting this sloppy use might be its most important function. It cannot be stressed too many times, the word barrel is not the general name for a container of beer, it is simply the name for one specific size, and a large, uncommon one at that (36 gallons). The general words are **cask** for traditional beer and **keg** for brewery-conditioned beers and lagers. Nothing demonstrates a cellarman's, or any other bar worker's, lack of proper training than this verbal confusion of barrel with cask – an employer interviewing any prospective new staff member could do worse than to make the first question require a response needing this choice of term. There is more on the naming of casks in a later chapter, for now let us start a new movement: CAMTRUC, the Campaign for The Correct Use of Cask!

Brewing real ale

WHAT IS REAL ALE? It may seem an unnecessary question in a book on cellar work, but just for any readers with holes in their knowledge, here is a brief refresher. The simple answer is that it is beer, but with certain special characteristics. So the first task is to describe the production of beer itself. Making beer is essentially a series of industrial-scale cooking operations. Four ingredients are involved – malt, hops, water and yeast – and as any good cook will know, their quality is all-important.

Malt is malted barley, supplied to the brewer by specialist maltsters (who also supply such diverse industries as whisky distillers, vinegar makers and the bakery and confectionery trades). To make malt, grains of barley are kept moist and warm for a few days, encouraging them to sprout – to start to grow as nature intended – then this growth is cut short by heating the barley in a kiln. Starting to shoot the barley seed, which is mainly a store of starch to feed the growing seedling, produces enzymes that break down starch into sugars (mainly maltose), both the sugars and the enzymes are essential to the brewer.

Hops, although green in colour, are flowers. They grow in clusters on the hop bine, a vigorous climbing plant distantly related to cannabis. These flowers and the seeds within them contain an extraordinarily complex mixture of aromatic compounds that are used to impart the unique flavour and aroma to beer. The choice of hop variety or varieties and how they are used has dramatic effects on the subsequent beer style.

Water is an obvious ingredient but in this instance its trace ingredients are the important factors – using pure distilled water would produce a totally insipid, unpalatable brew. Some hardness is needed, though not too much and less for lagers and stouts than bitters. Some sulphate content is considered by many to be very advantageous (the ground water of Burton-on-Trent has a high calcium sulphate level, which gave Burton beers the traditional sulphurous tinge in their aroma). Bacterial sterility, although desirable, is not a big concern since all the beer is boiled before going to the fermenting vessels. However, chemical contamination can be serious – chlorinated hydrocarbons and nitrate fertiliser run-off are especially bad. As a final point it should be remembered that water used in brewing is always referred to as **liquor**.

Yeast is a fungus, an oval, single celled organism. Each cell is microscopic, only about 10μm (millionths of a metre) in diameter – to get some appreciation of this, consider that just one gram of yeast will contain over five *billion* cells! All ales are brewed with one species of yeast with the scientific name *saccharomyces cerevisiae*. However, much as all dogs are of the species *canis* but have huge superficial differences all brewers' yeasts vary and many brewers guard and propagate strains that have been bred over many years.

With this set of ingredients the beer can be made. Malt is ground ('cracked' in the brewers' terminology) into a rough powder, now called GRIST that looks like an extremely coarse, wholemeal flour. A large, round vessel, called the **mash tun** is filled to a depth of a metre or more and hot liquor (at about 65–70°C) is poured in to create the **mash**, which resembles a huge vat of porridge. After steeping for an hour or two in the mash tun, the liquid, now full of sugary extract from the malt (and having acquired the name of **wort**) is strained off into the **copper**.

The copper is simply a very big kettle. As soon as the wort is in the copper the hops are added and the mixture is boiled very vigorously, extracting the oils and resins from the hops. At the end of the boil the liquid – now **hopped wort** – is run off through a cooler into fermenting vessels.

Once in the fermenter the initial inoculation of yeast is added, usually in the form of a large bucket of liquid yeast slurry that will have been skimmed from a previous brew. This process is known as **pitching** the yeast. The yeast finds the sugary, warm wort a wonderful medium in which to grow and it multiplies rapidly, consuming the malt sugars and excreting its waste products, alcohol and carbon dioxide (plus smaller quantities of many other complex chemicals that add to the flavour profile of the finished beer). After a few days the fermentation slows as the sugars are used and the alcohol level builds up; within about a week the final product, beer, is ready to be racked off from the fermenter.

Only now does the production of real ale differ from any other beer. Although the main fermentation has now finished and the vast bulk of the yeast is in a frothy head on the top of the beer, the beer below still contains billions of live yeast cells. For brewery-processed beers this remaining yeast is filtered out and the beer goes on to many more operations before leaving the brewery. To produce real ale a proportion of these cells must be kept alive and transferred with the beer into the casks that will eventually be delivered to the end user's cellar. These relatively few cells will continue to ferment slowly giving the famous **secondary fermentation in cask** that real ale is all about. Managing this fermentation and its effects on the beer is one of the main requirements of cellarmanship. Many chapters of this work describe these aspects in detail, and throughout the terms 'cask-conditioned beer' and 'real ale' are used interchangeably.

ETYMOLOGICAL NOTE: *CAMRA coined the neologism 'real ale' and it is now part of our language after being officially accepted by the Oxford English Dictionary. In the current full edition the entry reads:*

real ale, a name for draught (or bottled) beer brewed from traditional ingredients, matured by secondary fermentation in the container from which it is dispensed, and served without the use of extraneous carbon dioxide.

Cellar safety and hygiene

THE ENVIRONMENT of the pub cellar is not totally benign, hazards lurk and the cellarman must be keenly aware of them. This book will only touch on some aspects and any cellarman is strongly advised to become familiar with the current (extensive) legislation.

Perhaps the most common source of accidents in the cellar is the need to manipulate quite heavy objects, often in cramped or awkward situations. Never try to lift, or even move, a cask without assistance if you have any doubts about your lifting capacity. Know your strength and do not be tempted to exceed it. Use leg and thigh muscles, not back muscles, to do the lifting and never swivel the body while lifting, nor try to lift at a reach. Small manual or hydraulic hoists are now readily available and, although quite expensive (typically over £500), when combined with modern autotilt stillages they can virtually eliminate manual handling in the cellar.

The cellar has a lot of liquid content and frequently wet surfaces: not a favourable location for electrical equipment. There should be no trailing leads and no simple power socket outlets. Any unavoidable electrical units should have fixed wiring with waterproof control switches, fed via earth leakage circuit breakers. Fixed metalwork such as stillages or shelving units should have earth bonding fitted; cellar lights should use exterior, waterproof fittings and have ceiling mounted cord switches.

Later chapters mention the safety regulations concerned with chemical substances (COSHH, Control of Substances Hazardous to Health). These are extensive and rigorously enforced. Chemicals in the cellar are primarily cleaning materials, which should be kept in their own, marked, cupboard and always in the manufacturers' original containers. Never decant anything into any other receptacle and never use any glass or cup to measure out chemicals. Follow the makers' instructions and do not mix one with another. Avoid cleaners coming into contact with any aluminium containers; some varieties can react with aluminium.

The cellar has to be kept tidy and scrupulously clean, it should not be looked upon as a general storage area for anything not directly related to the beer and its dispense. Although usually a well-controlled cool room, resist the temptation to use it as an extension of the kitchen larder, food has no place there. Spillages should be mopped up at once, not only are they slip hazards but open beer puddles are the chief route for the spread of wild yeast and bacterial infections – a puddle will develop a grey film of yeast almost as you watch. Cellar walls and ceilings should be washed down frequently (do not use any disinfectant with a pervasive odour) and regularly repainted with anti-fungal paint. The core of the cellar cooler heat exchanger should be examined periodically for build up of blockage by dust, dead insects etc. and cleaned out as necessary. Progressive blocking of the core can lead to the heat exchanger icing up.

A particular hazard in pub cellars is the presence of pressurised gases, especially high pressure carbon dioxide. Carbon dioxide cylinders contain the gas held in liquid form by virtue of high pressure, more than 50 times atmospheric. This pressure increases rapidly with the cylinder's temperature, at 50°C it will be more than 150 atmospheres and above this, the cylinder's safety bursting disc will rupture. This is a violent event: a very loud bang followed by a roar as the cylinder's contents escape in a few seconds. To anyone who has never experienced it, it is a very disconcerting thing. Do not approach the cylinder until all noise ceases and do not touch it with bare hands as it will now be very cold. If the release was indoors, do not enter the room; open all possible doors and allow the room to ventilate for a considerable time – carbon dioxide in high concentration can cause unconsciousness without prior warning symptoms.

When connected for use, carbon dioxide cylinders must be upright and they must be secured in position with straps, a frame or a cradle. Full cylinders awaiting dispense may be stored horizontally but must be wedged or restrained to prevent rolling. Empty cylinders should have their valves left open. Never leave cylinders in direct sunlight – a ruptured disc will almost certainly result. Do not carry cylinders loose in a car or its boot.

Any gas systems, reducing valves, regulators, pumps, air separators, etc. should never be tampered with and should be maintained only by the suppliers' representatives. Never make any attempt to interfere with the central 'spear' of a keg, there have been fatalities from spears living up to their name.

Always stop up an emptied cask immediately with a cork bung and drive the hard **spile** right in. There are three practical reasons for this: a closed cask stays sweet longer, making it less of a problem to clean and sterilise at the brewery; an open cask is almost sure to leak some dregs onto the cellar floor; and it is also a courtesy to the drayman, who does not appreciate the **lees** (dregs) running down his shirt-front. Empties should be removed from the stillage at once and stored on end (preferably outside), or, if there is no room to stack them, they should have their taps removed, be stopped up and then 'up-set' on the stillage so that they may be recognised at a glance.

The British Beer and Pub Association (BBPA, formerly the Brewers' Society) publish a number of codes of practice on various aspects of cellar work and also two safety manuals, *Safety in Pubs (1994)* and *COSHH Regulations (1996)*. These can all be ordered via the association's website at: www.beerandpub.com.

Cask sizes

THE MOST IMPORTANT FACTOR in ensuring that real ale is consistently served at its prime is choosing the correct cask size to suit the volume of trade.

All but the smallest brewers supply their beers in a selection of cask sizes without any price differentials. This practice encourages the retailer to select sizes best suited to his trade. Unfortunately, a number of factors have reduced the available size range considerably over the last couple of decades. Smaller sizes have been phased out on economic grounds – handling and labour costs are broadly the same for any sized cask but the returns are obviously less. The larger sizes have mostly been eliminated by modern health and safety considerations (consider manhandling a 54 gallon, wooden hogshead, weighing over 400kg, into position in a cramped cellar).

Traditional cask sizes are all derived as fractions or multiples of the 36-gallon barrel, the brewers' historical standard of measurement. The introduction has already discussed the ubiquitous semantic confusion involved with 'barrel' so below we list all the cask sizes, current or antique, and the way to refer to them:

Pin 4½ gallons. Once a very useful size for the myriad of tiny beer houses and back-street pubs that are long gone, it also had a place for barley wines or old ales sold directly from a bar counter.
It is now almost purely of historic interest, although a number of brewers have recently (and commendably) reintroduced pins into their inventory. Current developments in cask manufacture (see next chapter) could make it more economic for other brewers to follow suit. Meanwhile, pin-sized containers do still survive in two other forms, the plastic bag-in-a-box Polypin, discussed later in this chapter, and the rigid cider Polycask.

Firkin 9 gallons. Now the regular cask size for the vast majority of small brewers, it is favoured by licensees as being, at 50kg, amenable to single-handed manoeuvring. It is often just referred to as 'a nine.'

Kilderkin 18 gallons. The other common size, for faster selling beers, it is usually called a 'kil' or 'an eighteen.'

Barrel 36 gallons. Half a century ago most draught beer arrived in barrels, wooden ones at that; now this large size, although still available from some breweries, is a rare sight on any dray. Nevertheless it is still the unit of volume used by many breweries to measure production or trade. For example, when valuing a pub, the surveyor will want to know the sales, calculated back to notional barrels per annum. Brewing plant is also conventionally measured in barrels – a 10-barrel mini brewery can make 360 gallons of beer at each brew. The excise duty formerly levied on a barrelage measure is now assessed in hectolitres.

Hogshead 54 gallons. The largest cask used in modern times, it is now effectively only of historic interest.

The introduction of the metric system into the brewing industry has produced another set of sizes that are now used by a number of breweries. The two sizes likely to be seen are 50 litres (about 11 gallons) and 100 litres (about 22 gallons) No names have been coined for these sizes, although they are often referred to by their gallon equivalent, as in 'an eleven,' rather than their metric volume. Even more oddly, many of the breweries using them still price their beer by the 36-gallon barrel (though they may not even possess one) and then price each metric container by its approximate gallon ratio. Just to complete the confusion of container sizing, a few brewers, particularly but not exclusively in Scotland, also use a 10 gallon-sized cask in place of the firkin.

The traditional cask names and the word cask itself, are used only when referring to cask-conditioned ales. Keg beers, lagers and processed ciders come in the same sizes (also commonly in 10-gallon containers) but these are always known as either **kegs** or **tubs**. In the smaller sizes kegs are usually straight sided rather than the traditional bellied cask shape.

Finally, the **Polypin** referred to above, deserves a mention. This is a collapsible plastic bag within a cardboard box with a dispensing tap already fixed. It holds some four to five gallons. Polypins were developed for the take-home trade but are not really suitable for cask-conditioned beer since they are difficult to vent satisfactorily – see the chapter on spiling. Their ideal use is for racked-off bright beer for quick consumption at outside events. Some breweries with retail shops often have even smaller two-gallon sizes, variously referred to an mini-pins, piggins and other pet names.

Cask types (including plastic)

For centuries, casks were all wooden (oak), the product of the cooper's trade, but these are now but a memory (see appendix 1). The usual cask today is metal, either aluminium or stainless steel.

At first, aluminium was the most popular replacement for wood but several factors have led to stainless steel becoming the most common. Aluminium reacts with some cleaning materials (caustic varieties) and so often casks had to be coated internally with an epoxy type resin. Also, because aluminium is relatively easy to melt and has a reasonable value as a raw material these casks are attractive to organised crime with a great number having been stolen and turned back into ingots.

Recently a totally new candidate appeared – the plastic cask. This often brightly coloured alternative to the metal cask offers the brewer several advantages: it is lightweight, easy to clean and, above all, costs less than a quarter of the stainless version. They are currently available only in one rather odd size, 43.5 litres (approximately 9.5 gallons) so have quite a large head space when 'full' but this is not a new problem for brewers, casks have always been made somewhat oversized. The manufacturers are in the process of revising the moulds to produce a more normal firkin volume and, more importantly, intend to introduce a pin-sized version. This could be economically attractive for many brewers.

For the cellarman, however, they do present some real problems of their own, but given the economics driving their introduction, it is likely that they will become commonplace and the cellarman will need to solve them. Some of the difficulties experienced by a small sample of early users are:

- Their light weight can cause problems with some varieties of self-tilting stillage and, with gravity dispense, a near-empty cask becomes so light that it will move with the operation of the tap.

- As may be expected plastic casks are somewhat less durable than metal. Being moulded in several sections and then glued, cases of the seams splitting have been seen, as well as cracking near the bung hole (presumably provoked by the blows of driving in the **shive**). There have also been reports of both keystones and shives being blown out of un-vented casks.

- The biggest problem is with stillaging and tapping. The surfaces of the cask are very smooth and slip easily on the chocks. This is exacerbated by the 'springy' nature of the plastic that causes the whole cask to bounce when being **spiled** or tapped. Using a metal tap and spiling tool and the heaviest mallet is recommended. Employing v-shaped cradles rather than individual chocks largely solves the slipping problems, although one user recommends patches of sandpaper stuck to the surface of the chocks.

- As the plastic is a very good thermal insulator, external forms of cooling are ineffective – of course the insulating properties could be an advantage in some circumstances.

- The top and bottom heads are made from the same mould, so the bottom head has a 'false,' blanked off, keystone ring; cases have been reported of careless users attempting to tap a cask through this end, both losing the beer and ruining the cask.

No doubt more types will soon appear as other manufacturers come into the market and many of these relatively minor problems will be ameliorated by design refinements. Until then the plastic cask will present the cellarman with just that little extra challenge.

Choosing the right sized cask

AFTER A CASK has been vented, settled and started in service, air is drawn into the cask to replace the beer drawn off. The oxygen in this air is taken up by the beer, causing oxygenation of flavour compounds and allowing growth of any aerobic yeasts or bacteria that may be present. Spores of these spoilage organisms are drawn in with the air and settle on the surface of the beer in the cask. The carbon dioxide, dissolved in the beer and giving it its 'condition', starts being lost through the exposed surface of the beer. All these detrimental mechanisms continue inexorably while the cask is in service, and lead eventually to beer that is flat and sour. Good cellarmanship can aim only to minimise these effects. With proper care, cellarmanship can ensure an excellent pint from start to finish of the cask.

The rates of these changes are influenced by many factors, including temperature, cleanliness, type and strength of the beer. Perhaps most important, however, is the combination of cask size and rate of beer usage.

The reason for this is that most of the changes depend upon the ratio of the volume of the beer to its surface area – the changes act through the surface but affect the bulk of the beer, so the smaller surface a given volume of beer presents to the air the longer it will last. Thus, the last four and a half gallons in the bottom of a barrel will deteriorate much more quickly than the same amount in a full pin. Figure 1 shows how the ratio of the area to volume in an emptying firkin increases dramatically over the last few pints.

It is because souring and spoilage derives from the surface of the beer and only gets down to bulk beer quite slowly that a cask can be perfect up until the last couple of pints (which is when the beer surface reaches the tap), which are suddenly 'off' and rightfully

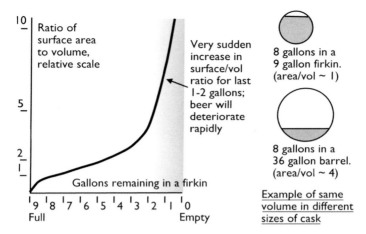

Figure 1 Rapid increase in surface area as a cask empties

rejected by the customer. In general, with two casks of differing sizes, emptying in the same time (i.e. at differing rates), then the beer in the larger will keep better. Conversely, when emptying at the same rate (i.e. in differing times), then the beer in the smaller will be the best.

With ordinary milds and bitters choose a cask size such that the beer lasts no more than two days. Strong bitters can stand three and barley wines or strong old ales will normally last nearly a week. High temperatures, bad hygiene and over-venting will reduce these times, while scrupulous cellar work – maximising hard spiling, keeping the air clean and the temperature correct – can extend them. The **demand valve** described in a later chapter will also extend this shelf life but their use presents other problems; the correct approach is to match the cask sizes and number of beers to the outlet's sales.

Where there are two dispense points for the same beer, it is always best to use a single cask with a double-ended tap (or a Y-connecter in the beer lines). This not only allows a bigger cask to be used up in the same time as two smaller ones but it also saves on stillage space, enabling more of the beer stock to be stillaged at any one time. The disadvantage, of course, is that both pumps go out of service at once.

Receiving and record keeping

NORMALLY THE CELLARMAN does not get involved in the actual delivery of the beer, the draymen will unload the casks and drop them into the cellar. It is the cellarman's task, however, to ensure that there is adequate clear space in the cellar to accommodate the casks, that there are no dangers or obstructions to the slide and that the empties are to hand, sorted and ready to load (draymen often need some persuasion to remove as many casks as they bring). It is also most important to ensure that all access flaps are secured and safely locked after each delivery. Access areas, where casks may be rolled up to the cellar entrances, should be kept entirely clear and clean.

Before accepting a delivery, check that the correct beers and cask sizes as ordered are present. Check the cask labels to ensure that there are no problems with beers having inadequate 'sell-by' dates.

As the casks are being delivered, check for any signs of leakage, try to reseat a weeping shive or keystone with attention from the mallet. If in any doubt either reject the cask or note the presence of a possible problem on the drayman's copy of the delivery note.

Casks are often delivered in a very muddy state (one wonders what they do with them at the brewery…), it is good practice to hose them down before they are stillaged (take care not to wash off any identifying labels).

Cellar activities should be methodical; part of the regimen should be record keeping. Ideally, each new cask should have a history sheet attached to show when it was stillaged, vented, when it became quiet and ready to serve, etc. This is a counsel of perfection that is rarely achieved; in practice the exigencies of a busy cellar usually preclude such thoroughness. Some logging, however, is essential, at the very least casks that are next to go on service should be prominently marked and all the staff should be aware of the marking significance. A middle course adopted by some diligent cellarmen is to record casks in a 'cellar book' (which these days, with advantage, may well be a virtual book on a convenient PC. This enables the records to be simply integrated into a spreadsheet to give stock usage statistics).

A number of pubs and bars now have EPOS (electronic point of sale) tills incorporating flowmeters in the beer lines. These can then produce records that show exactly what **ullages** were achieved from each cask.

Each individual brewery marks its casks with coloured bands of paint around the centre section between the rolling rings. It encourages draymen to uplift theirs if the cellarman separates the empties into piles for each brewery. The coding scheme is based on three rings chosen from a palette of nine colours and is run somewhat informally by the British Beer and Pub Association. All of the schemes are listed and illustrated in full colour on their website: www.beerandpub.com. As the website shows, the scheme is not 100% foolproof – a number of breweries are unregistered and have chosen their own colours arbitrarily while others seem to 'own' a whole spectrum of colour combinations.

Stillaging and chocking

CASK-CONDITIONED BEER has to be set up into its serving position and then left undisturbed until the cask is empty. The cask has to be supported in such a way that it does not rock or shake. The normal way to do this is to support it on three points only. An alternative system that stands the casks on end is discussed later.

When casks are being set up in some temporary location, on a floor, a table or on a bar counter, then **wooden wedges** (**chocks** or **scotches**) should be used. A suitable size is shown in figure 2.

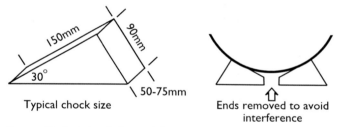

150mm · 90mm · 30° · 50-75mm

Typical chock size

Ends removed to avoid interference

Figure 2 **Typical chock size and shape**

The wedge angle should be about 30 degrees. Chocks of this size are readily made from odd off-cuts of ordinary construction timber and should be left roughly sawn. Although smooth, hardwood wedges look far more elegant and are durable, the rough softwood variety are more functional with a better grip. The cask must be supported on three of these chocks (not four), two at the front and one at the rear. For the maximum stability and grip chocks must always be placed with their *long sides downwards* (figure 3). It is important to ensure that the cask is lifted completely clear of the surface, to rest only on the three chocks. It can be

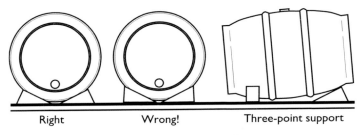

| Right | Wrong! | Three-point support |

Figure 3 **Cask chocking with loose wooden wedges**

advantageous to remove the 'nose' of the chocks to prevent the front pair interfering, particularly when chocking firkins. When setting up on a potentially slippery surface (plastic laminates are especially bad) a cloth or bar towel should be stretched under the chocks first; of course, all of the chocks must be on the same towel so that any tendency to slip is resisted by the tension in the cloth.

For a permanent **stillage** (also referred to as the **stillion, racking, horsing**, the **thrawlls** or, especially in Scotland, as the **gauntry** or **gantry**) in the cellar or in the bar, loose wedges should not be needed. It is better to arrange the stillage with permanently attached blocks. One common arrangement is to have two substantial horizontal beams as the basis of the stillage and then to fix to the rear beam wooden blocks with circular or V-shaped cut-outs, sized to fit the radii of the casks to be used. With this system the cask still has a three-point support, at the back on the horns of the cut-out block and at the front directly onto the front beam. The levels of the beams are adjusted such that, with the casks supported in this way, they are correctly tilted for the final serving position (see the later chapter on Tilting the cask). If less tilt is required at the start, then a simple block of wood can be inserted under the front of the cask. Another common form of permanent stillage is a brick or concrete shelf around the base of the cellar wall, usually between 300mm and 450mm high and a metre or so deep. In this case wedges would normally be used as if stillaging on the floor.

More and more pubs are now fitting proprietary steel stillage frameworks, frequently double height and with mechanical handling devices to load the casks onto them. These usually have auto-

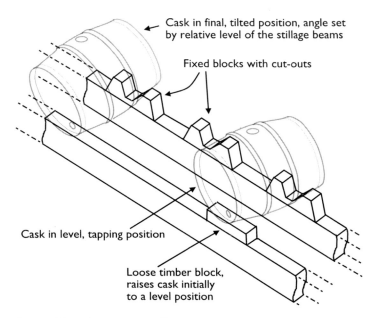

Cask in final, tilted position, angle set by relative level of the stillage beams

Fixed blocks with cut-outs

Cask in level, tapping position

Loose timber block, raises cask initially to a level position

Figure 4 **Typical permanent stillage**

tilting frames (also described in the chapter on cask tilting) at each cask position. The initial capital expenditure of these systems is high, several thousand pounds for even a modest house, but the two layer type, combined with these auto-tilting devices, is a very efficient cellar solution. Another useful device from these stillage manufacturers is the individual cask frame on wheels, these help in manoeuvring casks into tight positions, particularly under obstructions.

For pump dispense, whether the casks are set up directly on the floor with loose chocks or on a stillage, take care to tap in such a way that there is a suitable easy 'lead' for the pipes – angle the outlet to one side rather than straight down, even pointing the tap straight upwards may be best in cellars below bar level where the beer lines lead out through the ceiling.

Where enough stillage space is available, casks should ideally be put into their final serving position on delivery. If this is not practicable, then the casks should be stored on their side, bung (shive) uppermost and wedged to prevent inadvertent movement. Then, when moving to the serving position on the stillage, it is best to roll the cask to mix thoroughly and reactivate the finings and then to vent on the stillage in the conventional way. However, if there are time pressures and the cask has to be vented and conditioned first and then moved for instant service, this is possible but it must be done with the utmost care, keeping the cask completely horizontal and with no sudden accelerations in any direction. Several people are needed for this delicate operation but the wheeled frames referred to above would help.

Spiling (venting)

AFTER BEING FILLED WITH BEER at the brewery the cask is sealed with a wooden, or now more often plastic, bung known as the shive. The shive contains the build-up of pressure from the carbon dioxide as secondary fermentation progresses. Before the beer can be dispensed this gas must be vented off. In the centre of the shive there is a small recess, or in many cases a little coloured plastic plug; this is called the **tut**. The tut has to be punched through or **spiled**, to release the excess gas and to allow air (or any other gas) to enter as beer is drawn off. In many breweries the colour of these tuts acts as a visible code to indicate whether or not a cask has been fined.

It is remarkable that many experienced licensees still spile their casks without using any special tool – just a hard spile. Over the years, a vast amount of lost time and frustration must have been caused by extracting broken-off spiles or driving through others that have jammed. A hardened steel punch is the required tool and the cheapest form is a valve from a scrap engine. Ask your friendly garage for a good-sized one, preferably about 150mm long and with a 10mm diameter stem; lorry engines are a fertile source.

If the casks have just been delivered and set up, especially if you think they may have warmed during delivery, it is best to defer spiling for some hours until the beer has acquired cellar temperature. Otherwise the beer will be very lively so there will be a lot of waste and, worse, too much carbon dioxide will be lost, so the beer, when it has later cooled to cellar (serving) temperature, will be flat. In the normal cellar practice it is best, if space is available, to set casks up into their serving position several days before venting.

When time is of the essence – such as a beer festival or many outside events – venting must proceed at once and precautions can be taken. If there are two people available then one can use the venting tool and the other can be ready with the soft peg, held immediately next to the shive, to be inserted *instantaneously* as the tool is withdrawn. It is also advisable to cover the hand and the venting tool with a bar towel to prevent hops being sprayed onto the ceiling!

When it is expected that the beer will be very lively (some brews always are, others may be in warm weather), then the use of a proprietary venting peg with a controllable draw-off tube will save a lot of mess. However, as these have to be left in the cask for some time, if a very large number of casks are to be vented there will almost certainly not be enough to cope. In these circumstances, there is little alternative to creating some spectacular fountains of froth. Even so, despite appearances, relatively little beer is lost by this. The jet is all frothy 'head' and if collected would not normally amount to as much as a pint or so.

In the controlled conditions of the cellar, with a regular through-put of well-rested casks, beer loss when spiling should never be a serious problem, but if it does appear to persist then the controlled venting peg will eliminate the problem. In the past it was common for the beer blown off during venting to be collected in a sterilised jug and returned to the cask later. This is almost certainly a false economy, it is always bad practice to return any beer to a cask.

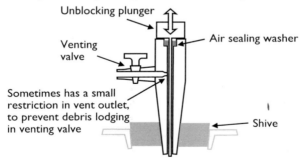

Figure 5 **Controlled vent peg**

As the tut will end up in the beer in the cask, it is wise to check its cleanliness. Before driving in the tut, inspect the shive for any visible mould growth (common on wooden items, and not normally to be considered of any concern) and scrape it away. The shive should then be brushed with a food grade sterilising solution.

After venting the cask with the venting tool, insert a **soft spile**. This can usually be put in finger-tight, although lively casks may require a very light attention of the mallet. Do not ever tap in a soft spile excessively, this crushes the pores in the wood thus negating its action. The best soft spiles are made of bamboo and are easily recognised by their short, stubby shape and the shiny, dark outer bamboo skin; the fibrous inner texture is quite visible. Unfortunately they are also the most expensive and hence are now less often offered free by brewers. The most common spiles now are made from coarse-grained softwood and are much shorter than hard pegs. If in doubt about a batch of spiles, put one to the lips and blow hard, a soft spile will be noticeably porous. Batches vary considerably in the porosity of spiles, so it is helpful to check your supplies from time to time.

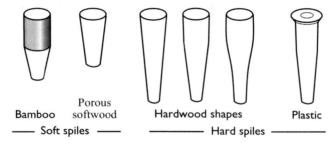

Bamboo   Porous softwood

—— Soft spiles ——

Hardwood shapes

—— Hard spiles ——

Plastic

Figure 6 **Common types of soft and hard spile**

With modern beers, many do not evolve much gas and do not give any indication of continuing to 'work' after venting (more's the pity, some might think). With these beers most cellarmen would now go directly to a hard spile after the initial venting operation.

After venting and inserting the soft spile, it is important to check regularly that the spile is not blocked. Remove the spile (at least twice a day, while gas is still escaping) and check that the spile hole is not blocked with hops or that the spile is not saturated with yeast. If you have plenty of spiles, fit a new spile each time you check the cask. Even with a cask that has been directly hard spiled it is wise just to ease this spile occasionally to check that no excessive gas buid-up has occurred.

A soft spile should only be left in a cask that is still actively producing carbon dioxide. As soon as appreciable evolution of gas from the cask has ceased, the soft spile must be replaced with a **hard spile**. Keep the hard spile firmly in place at all times that the cask is not in service, but withdraw it completely when the cask is in use. (If the beer is a low volume seller, it can be advisable to replace with a loose soft spile instead of leaving the spile hole fully open.) A hard spile left loosely in the shive can get drawn back into the hole by the air entering as beer is drawn off, blocking the hole and creating an airlock. This only becomes obvious in the bar when the handpump starts getting harder to pull and springs back after pulling. By this time there is a partial vacuum in the cask and removing the spile then will cause a sudden pressure change that will disturb the sediment and give cloudy beer. Should, by some error, a cask be put in service with a spile still in and an airlock develops, ease the spile out very gently, listening to the inflow of air and allow some tens of seconds for the pressures to be equalised. If a pump handle suddenly exhibits this symptom, especially just after changing a cask, and the cause is not a blocked spile hole, then it is almost always because the cask tap has inadvertently been left closed. In this case, gentleness is again the key: open the tap *very* slowly, or the sudden rush of beer into the line may cause enough disturbance to raise the sediment.

Where a beer is only in infrequent service – such as a cask at home or a firkin of winter ale on the bar – then the best practice is to keep the hard peg in tight all the time and just loosen it slightly to draw a pint and then re-tighten.

As already mentioned, an increasing number of beers today have very low levels of secondary fermentation (usually to the detriment of their flavour), so much so that venting them will release hardly any appreciable gas. These beers can, and indeed should, be hard spiled directly after venting, to retain what little condition they do have. This trend has reached such a degree that a number of breweries now issue only hard spiles to their customers or in some instances they issue 'semi-soft' spiles, which look like normal hard spiles but have a just detectable porosity.

The problem of using polypins with real ale was mentioned in the chapter on cask sizes. Should the cellarman be required to prepare a polypin of sedimented beer for sale it should be set into its final serving position and then rotated 90 degrees backwards about its rear lower edge, putting the tap uppermost. The tap should now be opened carefully to vent the beer. When the beer is quiet, has cleared and is in condition for service, rotate the box *very* slowly forward again about the same rear edge. If this is done carefully the sediment, which will have settled onto what will be the rear face of the polypin, will slide down this face and onto the bottom without being disturbed enough to give cloudy beer. Another (destructive) method is to vent the polypin in position. Cut an access hole in the top of the cardboard box and then vent by making a very small pinhole in the top of the bag. This is later sealed, when venting is over, with a piece of waterproof tape.

Before leaving this subject, TAP VENTING should be mentioned. This is a traditional practice, once common in the Midlands, particularly among outlets of the former Bass brewery. In this method of venting, the casks are not spiled at first at all but are tapped with the excess gas pressure present. Pressure is reduced by running off beer (often quite a large quantity), which then has to be used up in some way. The beer is then put on sale and only spiled later when some has been dispensed and the pressure has dropped to that of the surrounding atmosphere. There appears to be nothing to recommend such a practice and many reasons to criticise it, not least that it can result in beer with too much condition.

HISTORICAL NOTE: *A century ago, when the wooden cask was universal and shives were solid bungs without tuts, it was common for venting to be achieved by boring with a brace and bit. In many cases uncaring publicans would bore through any convenient part of the cask – a stave, even an end face if the cask was stood up! The tell-tale hole was stopped up flush with a hard spile before the cask was returned to the brewer. After a period of use some casks came to resemble hedgehogs that had been turned inside-out. Even as late as the 1970s the cellar manual of a prominent Scottish brewery warned, on several pages, that: 'casks should never be bored other than through the shive.'*

Automatic spiles

A NUMBER OF MANUFACTURERS provide so-called 'automatic' spiles or ventilators, of greater or lesser utility. These are distinct from the demand valves or cask breathers discussed in a later chapter. They fall into two main types: those that both allow the cask to vent off excess gas (i.e. acting as a soft spile) and take in air to replace the volume of beer drawn off; and those that only allow air (or any other gas) in, but act as a hard spile otherwise.

A well-known example of the first type is the **Race ventilator**, which is shown in figure 7. It is a small, inexpensive, moulded plastic device that is intended to be inserted into the spile hole as soon as major venting activity subsides and then left in place until the cask is empty. It has a spigot outlet that will take a drain tube to dispose of evolving froth but it is not advisable to use this feature as the device is not easy to clean and if filling it with beer/hops/yeast can be avoided, so much the better.

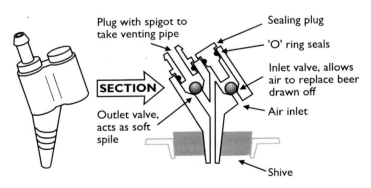

Figure 7 **The Race ventilator**

Operation of the ventilator can be seen from the section in the diagram, two very small (beware of losing them) ball-bearing, one-way valves act as both outlet and inlet controls. With the cask quiescent, both valves are closed and the cask is sealed. When beer is drawn off the partial vacuum created lifts the inlet valve and allows air to enter. Conversely if any fresh carbon dioxide is created this lifts the outlet valve and is vented off.

Generic diagrams of the inlet only type of peg are shown in figure 8. In most cases the valve is made from a moulded, shaped rubber sleeve with a slit in one end, this slit is held shut by any positive pressure but opens slightly under suction (the same type of non-return valve is found widely in keg connection heads). This type of spile is quite satisfactory for beer that is well conditioned

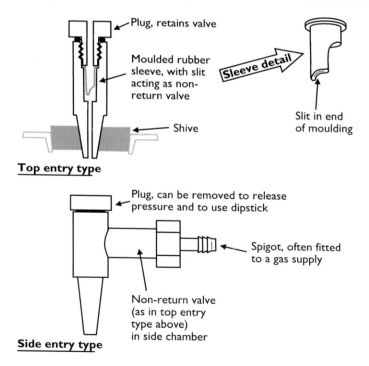

Figure 8 Inlet-only ventilators

and settled, however, if the beer is still working it can get over-conditioned by the build-up of carbon dioxide pressure that is not being released.

Both types of valve can be used with handpump dispense, since the pump will supply plenty of suction to overcome the small pressure drop across the inlet valve. However, neither type is recommended for gravity dispense. Tests with the Race ventilator showed that both inlet and outlet valves needed a pressure difference of about 0.75″ (2 cm) of water gauge to open. When dispensing beer by gravity this means that when there is less than two centimetres of beer above the end of the tap in the cask, beer will cease pouring. This is some three to four pints at the end of a firkin. A practical trial with a firkin showed that when beer had run to a very slow trickle, removing the ventilator produced three more pints quite readily. Although no similar specific tests have been conducted on the rubber-sleeved valves, they need a perceptible pressure difference before opening, so similar results can be expected. This is supported by anecdotal accounts.

Conditioning

WITH TRADITIONAL BEER, the term **conditioning** covers a series of chemical, biological and physical changes that occur in the beer from the time it leaves the brewery to the time it is served in the bar. Conditioning should not be confused with the **condition in the beer**, the phrase used specifically to refer to the amount of carbon dioxide in the beer; this is discussed in detail in later chapters. The main processes that concern us in this section fall under the subjects of: **secondary fermentation**, **dropping bright (settling, clearing** or **fining)** and **maturation**.

Secondary fermentation continues from the moment that the beer is racked into the cask at the brewery. It should substantially be over by the time that the cask has finished venting. In practice, a biological process cannot be turned off like a switch and some fermentation continues until the cask is empty.

During secondary fermentation, the residual yeast, left in the beer after racking into the cask, continues to attack the remaining sugars, generating more alcohol, carbon dioxide and flavour by-products. Secondary fermentation can account for a one or two degree drop in final gravity (0.1% increase in the alcohol by volume). A few brewers still add **priming sugar** when the beer is racked into the cask; this gives the yeast more food and stimulates a good secondary fermentation. Priming with sugar syrup was the general practice some decades ago but now seems to be dying out. Although this has eased the cellar work by making for less lively beer, the downside is in a reduction in the ultimate quality potential that beers can attain.

It may be argued that a second stage of fermentation in the cask is a needless complication – the process could be taken to completion at the brewery. However, since the secondary fermentation takes place much more slowly than the primary, and is in the presence of a high alcohol content, the resulting mix of digestion products from the yeast is different. This materially affects the beer's flavour. Furthermore, fermentation in the cask produces carbon dioxide, which dissolves in the beer, giving 'condition' in the beer, so appreciated by its drinkers. Without this natural condition the beer would be flat and lifeless.

Venting and soft spiling before the cask is put into service allows the excess gas, generated during secondary fermentation, to escape. Later chapters deal with the maintenance of the dissolved carbon dioxide level. During this time the cask must be left undisturbed in its final position, allowing the finings to coagulate the sediment, leaving the beer clear (**bright**), in the best case when the beer is brilliantly clear it is known as **polished**. Finings are made from isinglass that comes from the swim bladders of a number of species of tropical fish. These are almost pure collagen, which is dispersed into a colloidal state by steeping the bladders in a dilute natural acid (tartaric, citric or malic, for example). This slimy but invaluable, substance (in appearance similar to egg-white) causes all the yeast cells and any other solid particles to clump together and fall to the bottom of the cask. Usually, a proportion also rises to the surface of the beer. These two forms of sediment are known as the **bottom break** and the **top break**. It is in large part the top break sediment, floating on the surface of the beer that produces the cloudiness in the last pint drawn out of the cask. Fining is dealt with more thoroughly in a later chapter.

Under the heading of 'maturation' we may put all the other changes that the beer undergoes while in the cask. Among these are the slow interactions of the many fermentation products producing other chemical complexes, take-up of flavours from the dry hops added at the time of racking, elution of volatile substances by the carbon dioxide coming out of solution and the reduction of any oxygen still present.

The time required for conditioning and maturation is highly variable. Strong ales and barley wines will improve in cask for several months. An extreme example is the bottled Prize Old Ale brewed by Gale's, which is conditioned for a year before bottling and then kept in bottle for another couple of months before distribution. In the 18th century the best ales (by our standards exceptionally strong) were commonly kept in casks for five or six years before broaching. Conversely, modern beers of a low gravity – milds and light bitters – are at their best within a week or so of racking.

Keeping beer in the cask to come to optimum condition is expensive for the brewer and the licensee, tying up large amounts of capital and storage space. The result, all too often, is for beer to be put on sale before it has come to full maturity, this is **green beer**. There is also a noticeable trend among brewers to send out beers with less conditioning capability, beers that will settle and can be sold almost within hours of delivery to the cellar. The consensus of opinion is that these beers suffer in flavour. As a general rule, milds and light bitters should have a week in cask, best bitters two weeks while strong ales and barley wines will improve for up to a month or even more in some cases.

One practical problem for the cellarman is to know exactly how long a particular beer has been in its cask. Although the majority of brewers now put some sort of date label on their casks this is, unfortunately, neither universal nor are those that are dated all based on the same method. For example, most dates refer to the time of racking but in some instances labels can indicate the date of shipment from a depot or even the date that the finings were added. A number of brewers still mark their casks with **gyle numbers** (batch numbers that brewers use to designate each individual batch brew. The OED suggests gyle originated in the Old Dutch word for ferment). Others use letter codes, the significance of which are known only to themselves.

It is now usual for casks to carry 'best before' dates, in common with most foodstuffs. Although this seems laudable, it is something of a mixed blessing. In the first place there is, at least, a tendency for these dates not to be as far forward as many cellar experts would wish, and if beers are kept longer to improve maturity and a need arises to claim any ullage allowance then this will be refused for exceeding the date.

In a busy cellar the plethora of dating and labelling systems can cause confusion. It is advisable to use chalk or a marker pen to note, prominently, the delivery dates onto casks so that at least their time in the cellar will be known and the usage order maintained.

The time taken to vent off the excess carbon dioxide gas and to drop bright is also subject to considerable variations, generally longer for the higher gravity beers. As mentioned above, there are some beers that will vent and clear in as little as four or five hours while others can occasionally take as long as four days. When dealing with particular beers for a period of time one soon learns which brews are trouble-free and which ones are recalcitrant. As a generalisation, one should plan for most beers to have at least two days from venting to start of service and for very strong ales, three to four days.

Tapping

THERE ARE SEVERAL schools of thought on when a cask should be tapped. One view is that it should be done as soon as the cask is vented; a second is that it should be done a day or so before use and a third opinion is that a cask should only be tapped as it is required for service.

There are no overriding reasons to choose any one of these as being always the best method. Much will depend on particular circumstances and personal preferences. For continuity of service, tapping when venting needs a large supply of taps. It also allows some sediment to settle onto the tap end that will be drawn off with the first beer, leading to slightly more waste. However it is very much easier, tapping early, to handle any leaks that may develop; it avoids any danger of problems from disturbing the sediment in a settled cask and in general it needs less skill. At an outside function, early tapping may not be advisable as often it will present an obvious security problem.

Tapping only as a cask is required in service has the chief advantage of needing the least number of taps and when done skilfully, giving the least waste. The disadvantages are that skilled staff must be on hand whenever a cask is changed, there is some slight extra difficulty in dealing with leaks and there is always a possibility of disturbing the cask if the cellarman makes a mistake.

The middle course, tapping some hours before use, is the one advocated by many brewers. It allows for a degree of disturbance and it means that a systematic schedule can be adopted (for example, tapping the day's requirement each morning before opening).

Before tapping a cask, examine the keystone for any mould growth, scrape it off, then give the keystone a brush with a food grade cleanser. Remove the spile, make sure there is clear space to swing the mallet and hold the tap with its spigot pressed firmly into the centre of the keystone. Then with the mallet in the other hand drive the tap into the keystone with one vigorous blow. When holding the tap many people find it convenient to hold it between the fingers, behind the valve assembly and with the back of the hand to the cask head. Figure 9 shows this but after a few dozen casks everyone develops their own, most comfortable stance. Use as heavy a mallet as you can find – wooden, composition or rubber – preferably with a head of a kilogram in weight. Simple rubber mallets are often too light but rubber ones with internal loading weights are excellent and the best wooden ones are the round 'boy scout tent peg' variety rather than the square joiners' style. With a good mallet the experienced cellarman will be able to get the tap in place almost every time with a single blow. Never use any type of metal hammer, this will ruin the tap immediately.

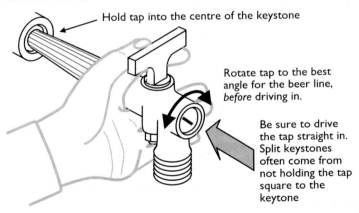

Hold tap into the centre of the keystone

Rotate tap to the best angle for the beer line, *before* driving in.

Be sure to drive the tap straight in. Split keystones often come from not holding the tap square to the keytone

Figure 9 **Holding the tap**

A few breweries suggest that the tap should be partially open when inserted but there is no evidence that this has any practical benefit and it just seems to offer more opportunity for waste and mess. After the cask is tapped, search for leaks in the tap or the keystone. Should either be leaking a replacement must be fitted at once (although if it is in a wooden keystone and the leak is only a slight weep it may well seal up as the wood swells with the wetness, so wait and re-inspect in a half-hour). The next section covers methods of dealing with leaking taps and keystones. Remember when tapping to give consideration to the direction of the beer line; angle the tap outlet to get the best fair run.

After tapping a cask that is to go directly into service, draw off about one third of a pint and discard it. The next third should be substantially clear and from there on the beer should be suitable to serve. Use a straight 'sleeve' or a parallel-sided highball glass for taking samples – the clarity can be much better judged. Casks tapped earlier should be tested in the same way before use, although slightly more may have to be drawn to clear the sediment from the tap. In any event if the beer is not clear and wholesome by the time two or three pints have been drawn, do not waste any more, begin an investigation into other causes.

Never connect a beer line to any cask until the beer has been tested, visually and by taste, *in the cellar.*

When the line is connected, always use a WASHER and **hop filter** (often combined into one) and tighten the **burr** firmly, but only by hand. With a good washer and an undamaged tap it should never be necessary to tighten the line with a spanner; thus subsequent cask changing becomes much easier.

Changing a tap in a full cask

FROM TIME TO TIME, when tapping a cask, the tap will be found to be leaky or the keystone will split and leak. In most cases, if the beer is not needed for a day, the cask can be upended and the matter dealt with; however if the beer is needed straightaway then the leak must be fixed without disturbing the cask. This seems a daunting task to anyone who has not done it before, calling up the vision of an expensive flood. In practice, the tap or keystone can be changed without either disturbing the beer or losing so much as a cupful. Follow these instructions.

- Hard spile the cask tightly. This is the key to the problem; it produces an airlock that will drastically slow down any beer outflow.

- If only the tap is to be changed (i.e. the keystone is all right), gently tap it from side to side and up and down and then, holding it into the keystone with one hand, continue to loosen it. It will become obvious when the tap is quite loose and only being held in by your hand. Should any movement of the keystone be noticed, use a punch to gently tap it back into place.

- Continuing to hold the tap into the keystone, take a cork bung in the other hand and hold it next to the keystone. Then, pull the tap straight out and slide the bung over and into the hole in the keystone. Do this in one movement and only a few teaspoonsful of beer will escape.

When the replacement tap is to be inserted, drive it in through the corked keystone, in the normal way.

Where the keystone has split it has to come out with the tap, so a little more care is needed. In loosening the tap you must also loosen the keystone so that they come out together as one. To do

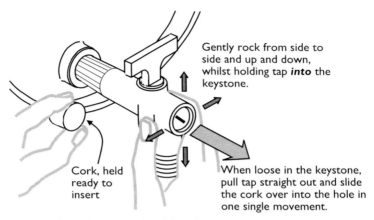

Gently rock from side to side and up and down, whilst holding tap *into* the keystone.

Cork, held ready to insert

When loose in the keystone, pull tap straight out and slide the cork over into the hole in one single movement.

Figure 10 **Changing the tap in a full cask**

this the tap is pushed in *very hard* while being rocked about. You should be able to see the keystone moving in its housing while still remaining tight on the tap. Inserting the blade of a screwdriver between the cask and the keystone with gentle leverage will help the initial loosening.

Once the keystone is loose in the cask but still gripped onto the cone of the tap, proceed as before, but in this case using a new keystone rather than a cork bung. A warning: if the new keystone is a wooden one check that it is round before beginning. If wooden keystones get even slightly damp they swell asymmetrically (because of the grain), becoming oval and then will not fit in the cask's keystone bush. Although the vast majority of brewers now use a single, standard size of keystone, there remain a few (especially in Scotland) that use an older, slightly larger size. Beware of being caught out holding the wrong one.

If possible, leave the new keystone for an hour or so before re-tapping. A new, dry keystone is more likely to split than one that has been softened by contact with the beer.

These operations are easy in casks that are full (the usual case, as leaks are not likely to occur other than at tapping time). In partially-filled casks the airlock created by the spile is not so efficient, so the dexterity required increases as the beer decreases.

Taps

THERE ARE MANY different types of tap in use, some with quite specialised applications. For well over a century all taps were made of brass or gunmetal, usually plain but sometimes chrome plated. Concern over the deleterious effects of heavy metal ingestion raised doubts over the use of any brassware in beer dispense (brass is an alloy of two thirds copper and one third zinc, occasionally with traces of lead). All brewers and cellar equipment makers decided that best practice would be to phase out these metals. Environmental Health Officers followed suit and will often react negatively to any brass goods used in beer dispense that they come across on an inspection. Yet, as far as the author can determine, there is no specific legislation outlawing brass taps *per se*. Many are still in use and it is hard to believe that they pose the slightest threat to health, but it is probably best to go along with officialdom and phase them out of your inventory (polished up they make an interesting bar decoration).

New taps are now available only in stainless steel or plastic. A stainless steel tap is certainly greatly superior to a plastic one in durability but, of course, it is very much more expensive, so the plastic alternative may make better economic sense.

For connection to a **beer engine**, a tap with a threaded outlet is required. The three most common types are: STRAIGHT-ENDED, TURNDOWN and DOUBLE-ENDED.

The straight-ended tap is the cheapest but it has two obvious disadvantages. It is not suitable for gravity dispense unless fitted with a special turndown racking adapter and, as it is driven in by its washer seating, it is prone to damage.

The turndown tap is the most useful for general purposes, as it will serve for both pump or gravity dispense. When used in the

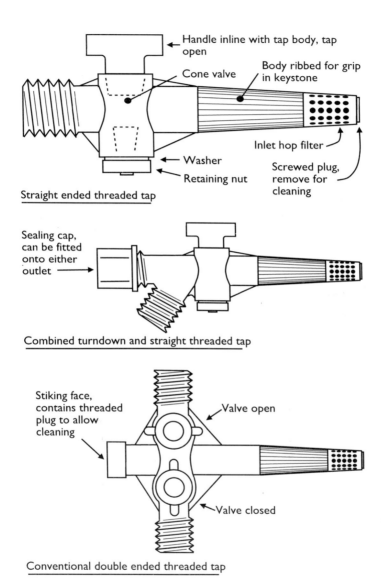

← Handle inline with tap body, tap open

Cone valve

Body ribbed for grip in keystone

Inlet hop filter

Screwed plug, remove for cleaning

← Washer

← Retaining nut

Straight ended threaded tap

Sealing cap, can be fitted onto either outlet

Combined turndown and straight threaded tap

Stiking face, contains threaded plug to allow cleaning

Valve open

Valve closed

Conventional double ended threaded tap

Figure 11 Some types of screw-ended tap

cellar it is usual to angle the outlet to one side, even upwards sometimes, to give the best fair run to the pipework. Many turn-down taps actually have both a straight and a turndown outlet with a blanking cap that can be fitted to the outlet not in use.

Double-ended taps allow one cask to feed two dispense pumps. Note that, with respect to the outlets, the open and closed posi-tions seem to be reversed compared to single taps. This is because it is the convention for the open and closed positions to be defined with respect to the cask end. With all taps, the closed position has the handle parallel to the cask end face. At the risk of stating the obvious, it is worth emphasising that beer taps with cone valves only operate on a quarter turn between full on and full off. Some newer types have a valve that toggles up and down on a cam oper-ated by a 'turn over' lever (similar to a free-flow font). These are usually known as FLIP-TOP taps.

A recent innovation in taps to be connected to beer pumps is the availability of taps with internal non-return valves, preventing any possibility of beer running back into a cask as a result of worn handpump valves.

The threaded taps for connection to beer lines come with sev-eral sizes of thread, some of which are hard to tell apart. This is a legacy from the nineteenth century when individual brewers or geographical groups of brewers developed their dispense systems without consideration for any standardisation. The traditional thread sizes are designated by letter codes. The most common are: Y, L, LL, M, S, and R. Of these, Y (Yorkshire) is the most common followed by L (London) and these are the only two now available as standard on new taps. In the last ten years this old system has been challenged by efforts to standardise with an entirely different thread system taken from industry, the ¾″ BSP (British Standard Pipe) thread and these are becoming very common.

Unhappily, the letter codes are not always marked on the taps and almost never on the nuts. If acquiring second-hand taps, try them first with the beer line tail nuts (or burrs as they are also known). Never have a mixture of thread types in the cellar. Inevitably the taps will end up in the wrong casks. One exception is that Y and L taps can coexist providing only L burrs are used.

For gravity dispense, the tap is known as a RACKING TAP. The best type has a fairly long, tapered outlet, smooth inside, which helps the beer flow in an unbroken stream. It is also much better to have what is known as a CANTEEN HANDLE to the tap – a long, single-ended handle like a tea urn. The turn-over toggle style is also good for gravity dispense – to minimise the chances of disturbing a cask a tap which needs the minimum torque to operate is best.

Another long, spouted tap sometimes used is a BOTTLING TAP. This has a very slender, tapering spout that can be inserted well into the neck of a bottle. Narrow grooves up the side of the spout allow the displaced air to escape. When a turndown threaded tap is used for gravity dispense it is good practice to screw a spare pipe tail on to it – this gives a much smoother stream of beer into the glass.

Wooden taps should be mentioned, if only to dismiss them. About the only use for a wooden tap is to give away to customers with off-sale casks if you do not trust them to return a metal or plastic one. If a wooden tap must be used for some reason, soak it in water for an hour or so first to let it 'plym up' and re-drill the inlet holes that are often only partially pierced through. Be sure that it is well driven in, as with the usual design the inlet holes barely clear the back of the keystone and only allow a trickle, or even become completely blocked.

Occasionally, taps can develop leaks. The cone valve that is the basis of most cask taps is an extremely reliable seal. Should the cone leak, with the retaining nut correctly adjusted, then the most likely cause is an internal scratch or some small particle separating the seal. In a metal tap the valve can be re-seated with grinding paste or metal polish just like an engine valve; this is less likely to be successful with a plastic tap. When dismantling taps, for cleaning or repair, keep the parts together in sets; the cones bed into the seats with use and are likely to leak if mixed up.

It should be stressed that cone valves do not need to be done up tightly by the retaining nut on the base of the cone, this is only to stop the whole assembly coming apart. Tightening the nut will not cure a leak. The tap should be quite loose, it lubricates itself by a film of beer between the cone and the body. It should become a habit always to pull upwards on the cone when starting to turn a

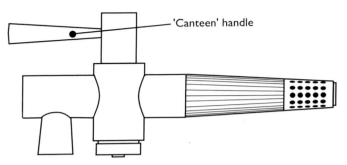

Typical metal racking tap

'Canteen' handle

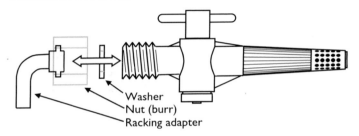

Washer
Nut (burr)
Racking adapter

Adapter, converts straight-ended tap to racking tap

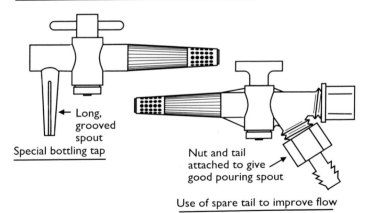

Long,
grooved
spout

Special bottling tap

Nut and tail
attached to give
good pouring spout

Use of spare tail to improve flow

Figure 12 Racking taps and racking adapters

tap and then to give it a slight press downwards when in the finished position. As previously mentioned, the connection of the beer line needs to be just hand-tight to be leak-free. If a leak does persist, check:

- **The washer**: washers can become brittle and crack. Traditionally washers were always leather, more frequently they are now rubber or clear plastic. The plastic variety do not seem to seal as efficiently as the old-fashioned leather or rubber. Leather has the same useful feature as the wood used for cask fitments: it swells locally when wet so that any incipient leaks almost always become self-sealing.

- **The hop filter**: sometimes the gauze dome gets nipped by the tap face or a stray strand of gauze gets across the face, preventing a good seal.

- **The tap face**: minor damage to the tap face can be taken out by rubbing on fine emery paper placed on a flat surface.

- **The thread types**: sometimes a nut will go on a few turns and feel tight only because the threads are incompatible and have jammed.

Tilting the cask

DO NOT WAIT UNTIL the tap flow reduces to a dribble or until the pump starts pulling air before **tilting (stooping)** the cask. Tilt the cask to its final serving angle while it is between a half and a third full. If possible, do this at the start of a break in service, in case there is any disturbance to cause the sediment to rise slightly.

Do not over-tilt. There is absolutely nothing to be gained by tilting more than to the point where the final curve of the cask is horizontal (about 12 degrees for a firkin, see figure 13). Too great a tilt will cause the sediment to collect around the tap and it will be drawn into the beer line. The overall end result will be more beer wasted and more line cleaning for the gain of a half-pint of indifferent beer. Figure 13 shows some experimental results for the liquid remaining in a nine-gallon cask when the tap runs 'dry' for a variety of angles of the cask. As this practical test shows, if the cask were left flat almost a gallon of good beer would be wasted but beyond 12–13 degrees little or no more wholesome beer can be recovered and the lees left in the cask will then be about 2½ pints.

There is a growing tendency among cellarmen to set casks to their final serving angle from the start. Whether this is practicable will depend on the type of cask, the amount of sedimentation and the degree of filling achieved by the brewery – some casks are completely full to the shive and would lose beer if tilted straight away. In any event, extraction of just a few pints allows almost any cask to be tilted without waste although for brews with very heavy yeast content it is best to be cautious.

It is important to tilt the cask in one slow, uninterrupted movement, just to its final position. Do not pull it up beyond its intended angle and then drop it back – this produces much 'sloshing' of the

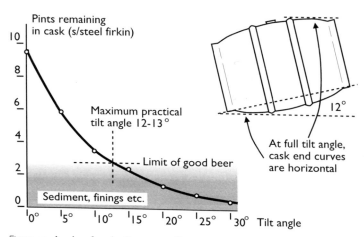

Figure 13 Angle of cask tilt versus ullage remaining

beer and will disturb the sediment. When tilting a cask supported on chocks it is best to lean over the front of the cask, lift gently on the back rim with one hand and slide the rear chock forward with the other hand, see figure 14.

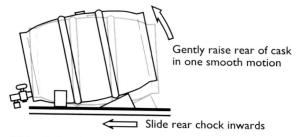

Gently raise rear of cask in one smooth motion

Slide rear chock inwards

Figure 14 Tilting by hand

There are a host of mechanical contrivances that have been produced in the past to aid stooping, ranging from complicated screw jacks to primitive, notched, wood ratchets. Now, a number of cellar equipment manufacturers produce a variety of **self-tilting frames** and stillage systems that solve the tilting problem completely. In a typical example, shown schematically in figure 15, each cask sits on a rectangular sub-frame, supported on rubber rollers that allow the cask to be rotated to bring the shive exactly uppermost, with the keystone/tap at the bottom. This sub-frame is hinged at the front end to a second supporting frame and held by biasing springs at the rear. The weight of a full cask compresses the springs to bring the sub-frame and cask level; as beer is dispensed and the cask gets lighter the springs gradually relax and the cask is automatically tilted up. The best versions have gas damper struts (as on a hatchback car) rather than just simple springs. These ensure that the movement is always slow and steady – spring only models can be prone to sticking and then releasing with a sediment-raising jerk if the hinges are not kept well lubricated and rust-free.

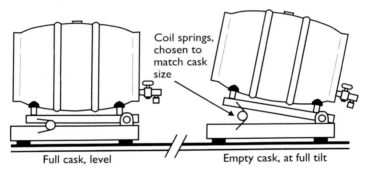

Coil springs, chosen to match cask size

Full cask, level   Empty cask, at full tilt

Figure 15 **Self-tilting framework**

These individual cask tilting frames can be incorporated into compact, multi-level stillage systems and usually have a mechanical hoist to make loading the casks both easy and safe.

Using casks on end

THE NEED FOR A STILLAGE is often an inhibiting factor when considering the choice between serving cask-conditioned beer, or just using keg products. Undoubtedly, putting casks on a stillage does use up a lot of space and the handling calls for considerable physical effort, something that the modern safety at work culture rightly condemns. This consideration alone can often put the use of normal cask stillaging beyond the scope of a single person. The answer to both the space and handling problems is to use **vertical extractors (cask syphons)**.

The syphon system allows a normal beer cask to be used on end, like a keg. Casks can be stood anywhere in the cellar by the draymen and then used directly from these positions. Vertical extractors, at one time just used in a few Scottish cellars, are now commonplace and can be considered as the mainstream alternative to traditional, laid-down stillaging. With the ever-increasing emphasis on safe work practices they may become the cellar system of choice. A number of manufacturers produce extractor systems and they fall into two, quite different, types. The first to appear was the rigid tube extractor.

The extractor or syphon is a stainless steel tube about a metre long and 15mm in diameter that is inserted into the cask through the keystone and extends to the bottom of the cask. At the top a screwed connection takes the beer line (same thread sizes as conventional cask taps). A valve is usually fitted near the top to allow the beer to be closed off, again as with a normal tap. The tube is inserted through a **body** section (often referred to as a 'venting body'), which has previously been driven into the keystone exactly like a tap. This body has a threaded upper part that can either have a sealing cap fitted when the cask is waiting to go into service, or an annular clamping ferrule when the syphon is in place. The ferrule screws down onto a flexible rubber or nitrile washer, which both grips the tube and provides an air-tight seal. To vent the cask there is a small cock in the side of the body connecting with the space above the beer. When installing a syphon system, you will need about three body sections and two blanking plugs for each of the syphon tubes in use. Figure 16 shows a typical rigid tube extractor.

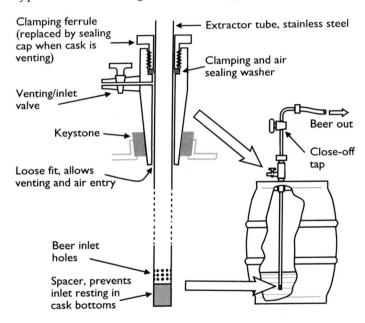

Figure 16 **Rigid tube extractor**

The spare bodies, closed off with blanking plugs, are used to vent new casks. A body is driven in and the venting cock is then opened slowly. If the beer is lively, a tube can be fitted from the outlet of the cock to a container to catch the fob. Take care not to have the fob collector below the level of the top of the cask, a situation that can give rise to a syphon action attempting to empty the cask. After venting, the cock should be turned off, which is equivalent to normal hard spiling. When the cask is put on service the plug is removed and the syphon tube, with its clamping ferrule, is inserted. It is usual to insert the tube until it touches the bottom of the cask and then withdraw it some 10–20mm to bring the beer inlet holes into wholesome beer above the sediment layer, clamping it there. Most makes of extractor have a metal or plastic spacer screwed to the end of the tube, in some cases of less heavily sedimented beers this spacer will be long enough in itself to keep the inlet in clear beer – the cellarman soon becomes used to where to position the tube for various varieties of beer.

A slightly dubious advantage of the syphon system is that beer can be served somewhat sooner after venting than with a conventionally stillaged cask. Since most of the beer clears from the top down, the upper part of the cask will often be clear some time before beer at the bottom, possibly within hours of being vented. By inserting the tube only part of the way (the clamping ferrule allows the tube to be set firmly at any depth), the top beer can be served while the bottom of the cask is still clearing. Traditionalists will object that to do such a thing is to be deprecated as this beer will be too young and 'green' but in practice, with normal beer types, no significant effects are apparent.

The second type of vertical extraction system, more recently introduced, is the flexible tube system, often referred to by the manufacturer's trade name, the Cask Widge. The venting body is broadly similar to that used with a rigid tube extractor and is used in the same way, except that the blanking-off plug just clips into the top with an O-ring seal. However when the beer is to be brought into service, the extractor inserted is a very flexible neoprene tube with a small float assembly at its end – figure 17 gives a schematic idea. As with the blanking plug, the extractor head and beer line connection just clips into the venting body and is sealed with an O-ring.

As figure 17 shows, the flexible extraction system adopts a novel approach to dispensing the beer that at first sight contradicts normal logic. The float, about 15mm in diameter and 40mm long, holds the beer inlet 10–20mm below the surface and beer being drawn off is continually taken from this layer just below the surface.

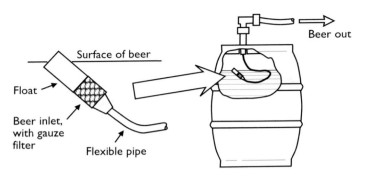

Figure 17 **Flexible tube extractor (the Cask Wedge)**

Traditional wisdom would suggest that this might be the worst possible point – on one hand it would imply that beer could be served very young, yet on the other it would seem that the beer being served is likely to be the most oxygenated and contaminated from the cask air. In fact neither turns out to be true. Trials do not show any young beer problems and by sweeping up beer from this sub-surface layer any oxygenation and contamination is prevented from spreading down into the beer below, keeping it at its best condition.

The flexible system has several other small advantages over rigid tubes. The tubes themselves are much easier to keep clean – the metre long steel tubes are quite unwieldy and need a purpose-made trough to allow soaking and washing and a special very long, thin cleaning brush. By remaining always just off the top of the beer a cask with a flexible extractor can be moved if necessary, with reasonable confidence of not having trouble from the disturbed sediment. There is one drawback to look out for; occasionally when the keystone is broached the inner portion does not totally break free but merely 'hinges' down. Although the float and tube then go in normally when trying to withdraw the float from the empty cask the 'hinge' traps it like the monkey's fist in the sweet jar, requiring the fiddly job of levering out the whole keystone to recover the situation.

Both syphon systems can give precise control of ullage. The amount of ullage remaining in the cask with a rod is determined by the height of the top holes (the first to draw air) in the extraction tube, above the end of the tube as it rests on the base of the cask.

As described earlier, with some trial and error, the positioning of the outlet holes can be varied to suit the amounts of sediment to be found in particular types of beer. With the flexible system, as the float assembly reaches the bottom of the cask it upsets and eventually part of the inlet filter either draws in the surface top break, to give a cloudy pint, or it starts to draw air. In a series of tests the average ullage in 18 gallon casks (of Taylor's Best Bitter) with a flexible extractor was 4.4 pints. In 9 gallon casks of a variety of beers, it was 2.4 pints (identical to the optimum for tilted casks, as shown in figure 13).

Some users of rigid extractors also slightly tip casks by placing a thin batten under part of the base, allowing the sediment to accumulate in one place. It is doubtful that there is any worthwhile economic advantage to be gained from this and there is the disadvantage that the casks are not sitting firmly on the cellar floor. It is not recommended.

A drawback of both syphon types is the difficulty of taking a cellar sample before putting a beer into service. This can be easily overcome either by using a large pipette to draw up a sample or using a plastic sample tube (available from cellar equipment suppliers) with a push button air valve, closed with the thumb, to extract a few ounces.

A few breweries have experimented with packaging cask-conditioned beer in converted kegs with syphons fitted in place of the keg 'spear'. With these, a special clip-on head is used for venting and for connection to the beer line. Providing the normal conditioning and venting principles are observed, this type of container is satisfactory for real ale although this development does not seem to have been greeted with much enthusiasm within the trade.

Carbon dioxide

THIS CHAPTER might be considered as the most important in this manual. Understanding the crucial part that carbon dioxide plays in enhancing a beer's palatability and then being able to control it is number one in the cellarman's job description. Should anyone have any doubt of this, just pour a half of beer, leave it in the cellar (to keep it cool) for a couple of days and then drink it – if you can – to experience beer without carbon dioxide.

Carbon dioxide (CO_2), a colourless, odourless gas, is the second most important product of fermentation. It is present in air in small quantities (0.037%, but increasing with global warming) and would be much more plentiful if it were not for the fact that, unlike oxygen and nitrogen, it dissolves readily in water. Thus much of the Earth's free carbon dioxide is in the oceans. The ease with which this gas dissolves is vital in producing the refreshing drink we know as beer. A primary aim of cellarmanship is to regulate the level of dissolved carbon dioxide in the beer being served. This is always spoken of as the beer's condition.

The amount of carbon dioxide dissolved can be expressed in a number of ways, for example as grams per litre, but in the brewing industry it is conventionally referred to in terms of **volumes per volume**. At cellar temperature and at atmospheric pressure, a pint of beer will hold just over a pint of carbon dioxide gas. What this means is that if, magically, the water could be removed from a cask of beer, a few pints of liquid (alcohol, sugars, finings, etc.) would remain and the rest of the cask would be full of carbon dioxide gas at atmospheric pressure. Only three things determine the amount of gas dissolved in beer: the temperature of the beer, the pressure of carbon dioxide at its surface and the recent history (in terms of a few hours) of any changes in these first two factors. If temperature and carbon dioxide pressure are held stable then the amount of dissolved gas is exactly determined and predictable; no more will dissolve nor will any be released, no matter how long the beer remains under these conditions. This is a very important concept, there are many who believe, erroneously, that beer left in contact with carbon dioxide will continue to absorb the gas becoming ever fizzier, however, the laws of physics say otherwise.

Temperature is a simple matter, keep it fixed at the serving/cellar value of 13°C. Figure 18 shows how the amount of carbon dioxide that beer will dissolve varies with temperature. Beer that is kept too cold, even by a few degrees, will be noticeably over-carbonated, while warm beer will have little condition and such flatness cannot be rectified by any subsequent in-line cooling on dispense.

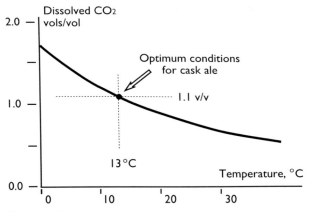

Figure 18 **Dissolved carbon dioxide versus temperature**

Pressure, however, is much more complicated and needs a short detour into the physics of gases. The pressure that matters is the absolute pressure of the carbon dioxide present. All other gases such as oxygen or nitrogen are irrelevant. In any mixture of gases, such as air, the individual gases act independently in producing the total pressure at a surface; each gas produces its own **partial pressure**. These partial pressures are in proportion to the proportions of the gases in the mixture. Thus with air the pressure of the atmosphere (1 bar or 1000 millibars, about 14.7 lbs per square inch) is made up of about 200 millibars from oxygen, about 800 from nitrogen and virtually nothing from the tiny percentage of carbon dioxide. In all considerations of beer and its condition, only the partial pressure of the carbon dioxide present is important.

Figure 19 shows the dissolved volume of gas for various temperatures and carbon dioxide pressures. This applies to all beers regardless of type or strength; indeed it is valid for any drink from lemonade to champagne. The diagram allows prediction of the state of beer that has been through any sequence of conditions. For example, if the gas pressure is increased at a constant temperature, the beer will absorb more gas and its condition will move upwards along the appropriate inclined temperature line. Alternatively, if the beer warms up at a steady pressure it will have to give off gas as its condition moves downwards towards the higher temperature line.

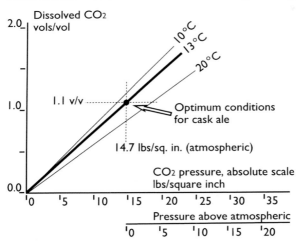

Figure 19 Dissolved carbon dioxide versus pressure

When beer arrives in the cellar in a cask, the only gas inside the cask is carbon dioxide (no air yet). The secondary fermentation that the beer has undergone since it was racked into the cask will have produced more carbon dioxide. Some of this will have dissolved and some will be present as gas, pressurised above atmospheric pressure but in balance, as described above. Venting the cask instantaneously lets out the excess undissolved gas. Then, because the beer is now super-saturated, gas has to bubble out of solution over the next few hours until a new balance is obtained. At the end of the venting period, provided that the temperature is right, the beer is in perfect condition. At this point it will contain just over one volume per volume of dissolved gas, the amount for 13°C and a full one bar of carbon dioxide partial pressure (that is, carbon dioxide at full atmospheric pressure, no air having yet been admitted to the cask).

Figure 20 shows the condition of a typical cask of beer during its life history in the cellar. On being delivered (point A), perhaps a bit warm from its time on the dray, it is placed in the cellar to come to cellar temperature. As this happens some of the excess carbon dioxide in the head space is absorbed, the condition increases and the pressure in the cask consequently falls until stability is reached at point B. Soft spiling the beer now releases the undissolved gas at once and the state of the beer starts moving down the temperature line to reach point C as the dissolved gas is slowly released. Arriving at C the beer is now quiet and in perfect condition to serve. From C to D the beer is on sale and it is the cellarman's job to make the path from point C, the full cask, to point D, the empty cask as short as possible. Note that nowhere in this diagrammatic way of presenting condition changes does time feature. C to D may be only a few hours or it may be a few days; increasing the time scale just makes the cellarmanship task harder.

As beer is drawn off, air enters the cask and mixes with the carbon dioxide already present. As the total pressure remains that of the atmosphere, the carbon dioxide partial pressure must drop as its proportion of the gas mixture reduces. The beer in the cask must now give up some of its dissolved gas to regain equilibrium. As the cask empties the beer's condition gradually moves down the line shown in figure 20. At first sight it might seem that, from a full cask, as soon as some beer is drawn off, the gas inside the cask will be virtually all air and the dissolved carbon dioxide will fall to nearly zero. However, as soon as air starts to enter and the partial pressure starts to fall, the beer will give off a substantial volume of gas to

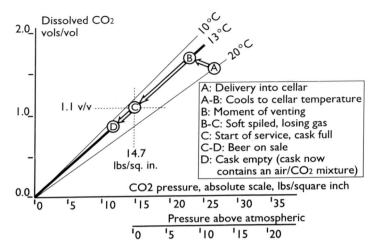

Figure 20 **A cask's cellar life history**

re-stabilise the situation. It is essential to retain as much of this carbon dioxide as possible within the cask, which is why the cask must be hard spiled at all times when not in service. Furthermore, two other factors help the situation. Firstly, it takes some time for the beer to give up its gas, if the cask is used up in a day or so, the beer never has time to catch up with the decreasing partial pressure and always has more condition than the pressure graph would suggest. Secondly, even though the yeast is taken down with the finings, in many beers a residual amount of secondary fermentation still exists, producing a small amount of fresh carbon dioxide.

The following sections look at some of the dispensing practices that directly affect the beer's gas content, for good or ill.

Top pressure

DURING THE 1960s and into the 1970s a collective madness came over the British brewing establishment. Brewery-conditioned keg beers and lagers were being widely introduced and as these needed pressurised carbon dioxide to give them (usually excessive) condition it was natural also to use this gas pressure to force the products up to 'free flow' counter taps for dispense.

The lunacy was to believe that such a system could also be applied across the board for cask-conditioned beer as well as for keg. How this **top pressure dispense** came to be accepted, flying in the face of physical facts and any objective taste trials is still a mystery. Possibly it was looked upon as embracing modernity, with the fast disappearing handpumps as symbols of a bygone era. Or perhaps it was just seen as a very short-term stage before cask beer vanished altogether.

In any event the impact on cask beer quality was totally disastrous, producing a beer that was massively over-conditioned and in many cases barely distinguishable from a keg product. Customer resistance forced a rethink and most brewers soon saw that the drawbacks of this method made it untenable and the handpumps reappeared along with the need for cellarmanship skills. The system is no longer installed, although there are still a small number old installations around and a few licensees, uninterested in the quality of their beer, who continue with this malpractice. For readers of this book this section should be considered as of historical interest only, included for completeness.

Another, somewhat disreputable, use of top pressure, although not for dispense, should be mentioned. If a cask of beer has inadvertently become over-vented and lacking in condition, some improvement may be obtained by taking it out of service and applying carbon dioxide at top pressure for a number of hours, allowing the condition to be re-established. This first-aid practice, which this book does not endorse, can only possibly work for good beer that has simply been allowed to go flat, it will do nothing to help beer that is old, oxidised or infected which should only be considered fit to become ullage.

Mixed gas

OF COURSE TOP PRESSURE is the required system for serving keg beers, stouts and lagers although modern practice now almost always uses a mixture of carbon dioxide and nitrogen, rather than carbon dioxide alone. Although a number of mixtures (60% carbon dioxide/ 40% nitrogen for lagers and 30% carbon dioxide/70% nitrogen for stouts and 'smooth' keg bitters are the two most common) can be purchased in cylinders, the modern method is to extract the required nitrogen directly from the ambient air. A compressor pumps air through a device known as a **molecular sieve**. There are several versions of these, slightly differing in their technology, but all with the same design aim. In one, the air flows into a chamber packed with many square metres of a proprietary plastic membrane that has the property of allowing oxygen to diffuse through (to be vented back to the atmosphere) but blocks nitrogen – the output is virtually pure nitrogen, which is stored in a cylinder, at a few atmospheres pressure.

Nitrogen from this reservoir is mixed with carbon dioxide from a normal gas bottle, via a number of ingenious proportional mixing valves to produce supply mains at all the gas ratios required. There are several advantages to be gained by using a gas mixture, rather than pure carbon dioxide, for top pressure dispense. The chief one is that the beer's carbonation level is de-coupled from the gas supply pressure. This allows a much higher pressure to be used, speeding up dispense (the slowness of pouring a pint of keg is often a tribulation to the real ale drinker waiting in line for his speedily handpumped pint). The high partial nitrogen pressure also helps in producing the characteristic tight, small-bubbled head that keg drinkers prefer. The obvious third advantage is a reduced use of carbon dioxide cylinders.

The 'free' availability of a nitrogen supply also suggests a number of other uses in the cellar. It is frequently used as the power source for the gas-powered dispense pumps now fitted by many breweries (see chapter on Gas pumps) and as the driving gas for ring main cleaning systems (where carbon dioxide is far from ideal because it reacts with some of the detergents used). On the real ale side of the cellar, pure nitrogen is sometimes used as the feed gas to a demand valve ('cask breather') purely to maintain sterility and freedom from oxygenation.

Air pressure

Air pressure is a dispense system employed almost exclusively in Scotland, where it is the predominant traditional method.

An electrical compressor keeps a tank filled with air at a pressure of between one and two atmospheres. This pressurised air is used to force the beer up to the counter dispensers (still in some outlets the beautiful, sculptured McGlashan fonts). One would expect that this should accelerate the detrimental effects of oxidation (as there is a higher concentration of oxygen at the beer's surface) but this is not readily noticeable. What is apparent is a definite increase in the condition of the beer, since the carbon dioxide partial pressure has been somewhat increased and none of the residual carbon dioxide being evolved is allowed to escape. In the 1980s there were attempts by some English breweries to introduce an air pressure system to dispense cask-conditioned beer from converted kegs, but these have not survived.

An obvious, somewhat ethical, problem with this method of dispense is that the customer has no simple way of knowing whether a font is dispensing a keg or cask-conditioned beer.

HISTORICAL NOTE: *The original Scottish system used an extraordinary Heath Robinson device known as the water engine. This unlikely device was introduced in Victorian times (1876) and was inspired by the cutting edge technology of the time, the water closet cistern. Mains water was connected to a sealed, cast-iron chamber; as this chamber filled it compressed the air above the water until its pressure was sufficient to feed, through a non-return valve, into the dispense system's air supply. When the chamber was full of water a float tripped a weighted lever that simultaneously cut off the water supply, opened a drain cock and opened a valve to allow more air to be drawn in. As the cistern emptied the float fell and reset this tripping mechanism, closing the air inlet and drain and opening the water inlet again – the whole cycle would repeat indefinitely while air was being used by the bar dispensers. If dispensing stopped, a diaphragm valve connected to the air system sensed when the system was up to full pressure and interrupted the float and lever system to hold the 'engine' in a static state, awaiting its next call to duty.*

These machines had wonderfully evocative names, redolent of the Scotland's engineering heritage – the Albany, the Laidlaw, Bishop and Babcock's Big and Little Wonders and the Allan and Bogle. There was even a design from the famous Gaskell and Chambers cellar equipment makers that was only introduced in 1946.

One can only speculate how twenty-first century water companies would view such devices.

Blanket pressure

THE EXPRESSION **blanket pressure** describes a number of systems for replacing the beer drawn from the cask with carbon dioxide, nitrogen or a gas mixture, rather than just admitting air. It is not a way of dispensing the beer, as in the case of top pressure, described above.

The acceleration in the various deterioration processes that occurs after a cask is half empty (when the remaining beer has a large surface to volume ratio) leads to the rationale for blanket pressure. The argument is that by excluding the air the 'blanket' would both prevent the beer from biological contamination problems and preserve the condition. Proper choice of cask size to suit the level of trade, good cellar hygiene and good cellarmanship make it unnecessary; use of blanket pressure is thus an admission of lack of foresight.

Nevertheless, there are a few exceptional circumstances in which it can be justified. Very low turnover outlets, especially ones with erratic trade patterns, may be obliged to use a blanket pressure system if they wish to offer a good quality cask beer rather than only keg.

In this instance it is vital that the correct equipment is used. In the past, many brewers would have suggested using an ordinary gas regulating valve, as used for keg dispense, set to a very low pressure – a tenth of a bar or so. This is not satisfactory on two counts. Firstly, regulating valves tend to be unreliable when set to the end of their range. The actual pressure of the blanket gas can be substantially above atmospheric, giving objectionable over-conditioning. Secondly, connection to such a valve makes no allowance for venting off any more excess carbon dioxide that may be being produced by the beer in the cask (no soft spile action), again resulting in over-condition.

In those rare cases where a blanket system has to be used, then it should be with the proper equipment, the demand valve, described in the next chapter.

The contamination argument also leads to another approach, particularly for casks in the bar, where it is said that the incoming air brings with it odours from tobacco smoke or cooking. The 'bad bar air' argument has an intuitive appeal, but there appears to be no scientific evidence of any tests that have shown flavour changes.

However, where there is doubt, or where these arguments are used as an excuse for not having traditional dispense or for using blanket pressure, then one answer is **air filtration**. After venting the cask, instead of removing the hard spile when the cask is in service, it is replaced with a small metal or plastic spigot. This spigot is connected by flexible tubing to a filter unit, normally mounted on a wall. This unit contains a sub-micron filter element (usually made from a cellulose type material, akin to cotton wool), which allows free passage to air but traps any organisms or spores. If an activated charcoal element is also included, most odour molecules will be removed as well. Several casks can be connected to one filter element. Commercial units are available from a number of bar equipment suppliers but a DIY version is well within the capability of the average handyman.

Where the bar air argument is the only worry, the air supply can obviously be improved by using just a length of thin tubing taken to an area of good fresh air, without the need to fit a filter at all.

Demand valve (the cask breather)

THIS SIMPLE DEVICE, often referred to as a **cask breather**, was introduced several decades ago, with the object of removing the unreliable aspects of the blanket pressure system described above.

The breather is a demand valve; it supplies carbon dioxide (or any other gas) at exactly atmospheric pressure *on demand*. In other words, when connected to a cask, it tops up the volume above the beer with exactly one volume of gas for each volume of beer drawn off. Unlike a conventional variable pressure regulator, which has no self-regulating feedback to control its output pressure, the demand valve is a servo-mechanism with the output controlled by feedback to exactly track the outside atmospheric pressure. There are no adjustments to set (thus none that can be mis-set) and no internal force balances to go out of adjustment. In this respect the design answers fully the first of the problems with normal blanket pressure. The second problem is catered for by the inclusion of a secondary relief valve, within the unit, that automatically vents to atmosphere any build up of excess pressure, in other words an automatic soft spile. There are a number of manufacturers but their operating principles are much the same, figure 21 shows one typical example in cross-section.

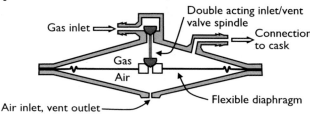

Figure 21 **Diagrammatic cross-section of a demand valve**

In the situations described earlier – the erratic and marginal turnover outlets – if a carbon dioxide, nitrogen or mixed gas replacement system has to be used as a means of ensuring that acceptable quality cask-conditioned beer can be sold, rather than keg beer, this is the only equipment to give a satisfactory result.

Figure 22 shows the valve's operation in supplying make-up gas to a cask that is having beer taken out by the dispense system. As soon as beer is drawn off the slight pressure drop in the cask, transmitted to the top of the flexible diaphragm with atmospheric pressure on the bottom, unbalances the forces on the diaphragm and it is deflected upwards, opening the inlet valve to admit just enough gas to restore the balance.

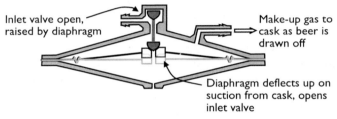

Figure 22 **The demand valve admitting make-up gas**

Figure 23 shows the device acting as an automatic soft spile. If the beer is still working and carbon dioxide is being evolved then pressure on the top of the diaphragm will increase, the force imbalance will now deflect the diaphragm down, opening the valve in its centre and venting the excess gas off to the exterior via the balancing air chamber.

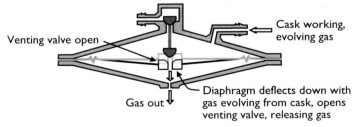

Figure 23 **The demand valve acting as a soft spile**

It is not worth using demand valves in outlets with normal sales volumes since it involves an unnecessary expenditure on gas and equipment. Furthermore, it can lead to lack of care in cask size control, with beers consequently being subjected to abnormally long shelf lives. With the breather, casks can be kept on sale for periods far longer than brewers ever intended, periods well beyond the sell-by-dates now common in the trade. The result is the beer, although still retaining condition and being protected from bacterial contamination, develops other unusual, 'old' flavours that with normal cellar practice would not have had time to appear before the onset of flatness and sourness.

A case against the demand valve can also be made on the difficulty of cleaning should it be contaminated by beer from an over-lively cask getting into the chamber above the diaphragm. This is certainly true, although the unit can be dismantled reasonably easily and the components washed; re-assembly needs to be done with some care. This problem can be avoided if the valve feeds the cask via a liquid trap (as used in compressed air systems or fuel systems). Note that one valve and trap can be connected to a number of casks.

In recent years, some brewers have justified their use of cask breathers more on the biological control rather than on condition control. In this mode it has been common to use nitrogen as the replacement gas rather than carbon dioxide. The companies promoting the system for these ends recommend its use for all levels of turnover. In these circumstances the nitrogen is usually free, being taken from the supply to the lager and keg beer mixed gas system. However, even with a nominally free resource, the shelf life argument still needs addressing.

Dispense systems

THE OLDEST, simplest and many would say still the best, beer dispense system is the direct use of gravity. A turndown tap directly in a cask stillaged in the laid-down position, could hardly be simplified to any lesser essentials. The development of affordable and efficient cooling systems, such as external saddles, has prompted something of a welcome renaissance for this traditional dispense. From the licensee's point of view, gravity service has no beer wastage, virtually no equipment to maintain and can provide an eye-catching focus for customers for whom it provides a near-perfect pint. Clearly a gravity dispense house presents no special problems for the cellarman but provides the novelty of performing his tasks in public.

Despite the attractions of gravity dispense, to a huge degree the system of choice for cask-conditioned beer is the bar mounted handpump or beer engine. In its earliest manifestations, two centuries ago, the handpump was mounted as part of the bar back fittings; it was only at the end of the nineteenth century that the through-the-counter, quadrant handled style appeared. Although most brewers made great efforts in the 1960s to finally cast them into oblivion, customer resistance, helped by CAMRA's campaigning, won the day. The handpump is now the iconic symbol of the British pub. So much so that advertisers of keg beers frequently include handpumps peripherally in their visual images, even though they are not related to the advertised products, since they recognise that they have huge customer recognition and appeal.

Mechanically, the handpump, or beer engine, is a very simple device, a generic design is shown in figure 24. A vertical cylinder contains a well-fitting piston connected to a piston rod that operates

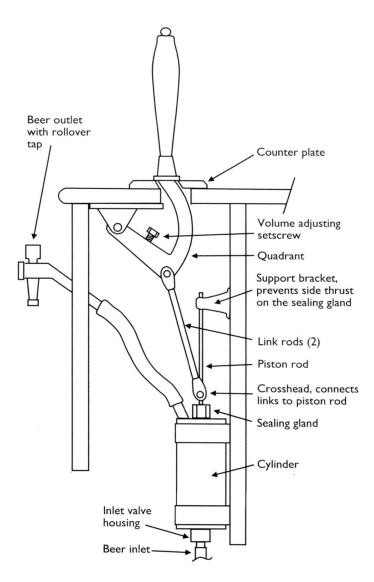

Beer outlet
with rollover
tap

Counter plate

Volume adjusting
setscrew

Quadrant

Support bracket,
prevents side thrust
on the sealing gland

Link rods (2)

Piston rod

Crosshead, connects
links to piston rod

Sealing gland

Cylinder

Inlet valve
housing

Beer inlet

Figure 24 **The classic style of a beer engine or handpump**

through a beer-tight seal in the cylinder top cap. The piston contains a one-way valve that opens if the piston is pushed down – allowing beer to flow through from the bottom of the cylinder into the top, this valve closes if the piston is now pulled up and the beer above it is forced out of the cylinder, through the spout and into the glass. The rising piston causes a suction below that draws more beer into the lower part of the cylinder via another one-way valve in the bottom cap. This valve retains the beer when the piston goes down again. Thus with the handle upright and the piston at the bottom of the cylinder, there is beer above the piston awaiting the next customer.

The rather oddly shaped quadrant is a segment of a circle centred on the pivot point. This design was adopted to provide a pump that fitted well onto the counter top, only needing one small hole through the bar top and with no visible mechanism. As the handle's motion is rotary and the piston rod's linear, the linkage between them cannot remain in line; to contain these off-axis forces, which would bend the piston rod and cause rapid wear in the sealing gland, a support bracket or brackets must be provided. Any steam engine builder would recognise this as the usual piston to wheel linkage. The volume of beer produced by each pull of the pump is regulated by the stroke of the piston and this is normally set by an adjustable setscrew as shown.

Handpumps can develop internal leaks for a number of reasons. If the inlet valve or its seat is worn, beer will drop back from the cylinder into the cask. These valves can be re-ground as with tap valves. A simpler cure is an external non-return valve – a later chapter describes these valves. If either the valve in the piston or the cylinder bore is worn the symptom will be low beer delivery for each stroke of the pump. If the adjustable stops cannot be set such that the beer engine delivers a full half or quarter pint for a complete stroke, then there is internal leakage around the piston. The pump will have to be stripped down. It may require only a replacement O-ring for the piston or a complete new cylinder/piston assembly may be needed.

There are many places in a beer engine where external leaks can occur. The remedy for most will be obvious to the practically minded. One common component worth mentioning is the piston rod sealing gland. On many makes of pump this is designed with several conical cork inserts; if through wear a leak may start, it can be re-sealed by simply tightening the gland nut slightly, compressing the cork inserts – one turn or less is usually enough.

Metered pump systems were introduced as another facet of the extraordinary anti-handpump movement of the 1960s and 1970s. They became particularly common in urban pubs and clubs of the Midlands and North, and, although less frequently fitted now, there are still many existing installations. The prime mover was usually a low voltage (24v) impeller pump, although many have now been replaced by gas powered pumps (see chapter on Flojets). The metering part of the system is an enclosed chamber, usually under a Custom and Excise seal, with an internal, moveable diaphragm. As beer is pumped into one side the diaphragm moves across and dispenses the measured volume (a half-pint) from the other side. At the end of the travel a change-over valve reverses the inlet and outlet for the next half-pint and the operation is repeated in the other direction.

The metering chambers are frequently transparent and incor-porated into the dispense font so that the customer can see his beer being measured out. Of these display types one is cylindrical (the Metronic) and another spherical (the Spheromatic). A third make, the Porter-Lancastrian, is always located in the cellar. As these are all sealed, proprietary systems there is little that the cel-larman can do by way of maintenance. Under no circumstances may the Customs and Excise seals be tampered with.

Many disadvantages attach to metered systems and there are few, if any, advantages. Despite being tested for accurate volumes they can still deliver short measure if the beer is lively and develops any gas break-out *en route* from the cask, which is problematical as there is no means of delivering a top up. Some outlets keep a full glass at each font for this purpose. For the same reason, serving a half-pint of a mixed beer or a made-up shandy is precluded. As the electric pumps are normally not self-priming they need some gas pressure to be applied to each new cask to start service; of course in most cases this gas then remains applied throughout service, thus ruining the pint.

Many metered systems also include in the beer pipework a **fob detector** such as the Cellarbuoy. This is a small, transparent chamber, like an inverted jam jar, containing a float. Beer flows into one side and out of a central point in the base – as long as the chamber remains full and the float is at the top. As soon as any fob or gas enters the chamber it collects in the top and the float drops, sealing the beer outlet and preventing the fob/gas being pumped further into the pipework. The float also, in some models, operates a switch to cut off the pump's power supply.

HISTORICAL NOTE ON THE SIMCUP PUMP. *When gravity dispense of speciality beers from a cask on the bar back was common, there was still a desire in those pubs where the other beers were being served from handpumps with 'tight' heads for the gravity beer to have the same appearance. The makers of the Simcup pump came to the rescue.*

As figure 25 shows, it was a small, quarter-pint handump that attached directly to the tap in the cask. The piston was driven directly from the handle via a rack and pinion. The beer outlet was a narrow pipe with the end flattened to make a narrow orifice. The pump action was wonderfully smooth – one finger could pull a pint with a perfect 'Northern' head.

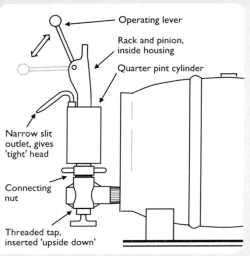

Figure 25 **The Simcup pump**

The author last saw one in use about 20 years ago, but would be interested to know if they are still in use anywhere – being made of solid brass would probably count as a death sentence in modern times.

Beer lines and their cleaning

THROUGH THE YEARS, since the introduction of the handpump at the end of the Georgian era, there has been need for a flexible piping system to connect casks in a cellar to dispense points in the bar. Various solutions have been tried, but there is now only one universal material – plastic, either MDP (medium density polyethylene) or food grade PVC (polyvinyl chloride). Such tubing fits the requirements ideally – it is strong and durable, lightweight, flexible, has a smooth inner bore (important for not leaving any crevice for yeast cells to colonise) and its transparency helps in checking for cleanliness.

Beer line comes in a number of bore sizes, the most popular today being ½" (12.7mm) although users should consider refitting with ⅜" (9.5mm) if possible, for economical reasons (see chapter on beer recycling for details of beer quantities in pipes). The lines attach to cask taps and pumps with a **tail and burr** (nut) connection. Figure 26 shows the parts of a line connection.

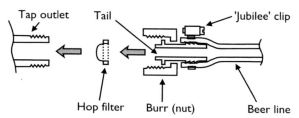

Figure 26 **Beer line tail and burr**

To assemble a tail and burr connection, cut the pipe end squarely with a sharp knife, thread a Jubilee clip of a suitable size onto the pipe and push it well out of the way. Screw the tail onto a spare tap with the burr to be used (this makes the tail/burr much easier to handle), then, hold about 5cm of the pipe end in a saucepan of boiling water. After about a minute the pipe will be soft enough to push straight onto the tail, do this quickly and boldly, the pipe will cool and toughen up in a few seconds. Finally, run the burr back down over the tail, position the clip over the pipe/tail combination and tighten it firmly.

Beer is as much a food as bread or meat and should be treated with the same regard to hygiene. Yeast, mould and bacterial infections occur with the greatest of ease. Treat the cellar as if it were your kitchen.

Whatever sort of dispense pumps are in use for cask-conditioned beers, the system must be cleaned at least once a week. Without question it is wise to make this an absolutely fixed ritual, at the same time(s) each week, to avoid any temptation to 'just leave it until tomorrow.' There are many specialised line cleaning liquids on the market, often, if you are a tied house, the brewer/landlord will specify a particular product. Regardless of the brand employed it is very important that the current COSHH (Control of Substances Hazardous to Health) regulations are observed – it must be safely stored, usually in a special locker or chemical store and you must have the safety data sheets to hand. Environmental Health Inspectors are very keen on the COSHH laws. The usual line cleaning method is:

- Have several clean buckets (preferably stainless steel) to hand. Fill one with cold water and the other with cleaning solution, made up to the dilution advised by the manufacturer – do not be tempted either to economise by weakening the mix or to make it too strong. Never save any mixed cleaning solution for use another time, always mix a new batch.

- Disconnect the lines from the casks, dip them in the water bucket and pull through water to drive out the residual beer, remove the tails from the bucket and continue pumping until the lines are empty.

- Place the lines in the cleaning mixture bucket and then pull in the cleaning solution. Leave to soak for the specified time, usually 10–20 minutes and then draw off enough to refill the whole system with a new charge of cleaner, again leave to soak. Do not leave cleaner in the system longer than recommended, it is somewhat corrosive and over time can cause etching of the pipes.

- After the second fill of cleaner has soaked, put the lines back into the clean water and flush the lines through very thoroughly until there is no trace of taste. Finally empty the lines of water and reconnect them to the casks.

Pumps and lines that are temporarily out of use should be left full of water and flushed at intervals to keep them 'sweet.' At intervals of six to twelve months pumps and any valves in the lines should be inspected for any wear, leakage or build up of deposits.

A number of cellar suppliers have introduced electronic and magnetic pipe cleaning aids. These are based on some good science: that magnetic fields can affect the solubility of some of the salts in hard water. Power station boiler feedstock has been treated magnetically for a number of years. However there is little or no evidence that there are any effects on the yeast and bacteria content, which is what concerns us with beer lines. The installations either involve fitting a coil around each pipe close to the cask tap end or clamping magnets around the pipes. The coil-based units are driven with a low voltage, variable, audio frequency signal from a small wall-mounted power unit. To recap, there is no evidence that any of these systems are worth investing in, the advice is to keep your chequebook firmly closed. The labour-free, self-cleaning beer line still awaits invention.

Taps must be cleaned between use although it is not necessary to dismantle them between every use. They can be left soaking in a weak cleansing solution until needed (make sure the tap is in the open position before putting it in to soak). Rinse through thoroughly with water before tapping into the cask. Taps can also be cleaned quite effectively in a dishwasher: put them in open, with the spouts down, in the direction of the water jets. At intervals taps should be dismantled and all the parts examined.

Leaks in beer lines are uncommon but can sometimes be troublesome. A leak sufficient to show visible beer escape will be obvious to find and easy enough to cure but often leaks only manifest themselves by a one-way action – leaking air into the system under the suction from the pump but then sealing and not allowing any visible escape of beer. The result is persistent and unexplained fobbing at the pump. If such a leak is suspected then it is best to study the pipework carefully while beer is being pulled: look for a tiny stream of bubbles being drawn along the line and then follow it back to find its source.

HISTORICAL NOTE: *As the handpump first appeared, there was only one known pipe system available to connect it – soft lead. Disregarding the toxic properties, imagine the labour of lugging several hundred-weight of tubing across a cellar floor each time a cask is changed. Even so lead was the beer line of choice throughout the nineteenth century and lasted until beyond the middle of the twentieth. As late as the 1970s one brewery's manual advised that '...these should be replaced...' implying that they still lingered on. When the poisoning dangers were recognised, reaction was hardly dramatic – first moves were to 'tin wash' the pipes, giving them an inner coating of pure tin. This was not a success as the tin cracked and was corroded by the highly caustic cleaners in use.*

Natural rubber, a wonder product at the end of the 1800s, was tried. Flexible, much lighter and certainly not as likely to cut short the drinker's life, it was however, disastrous for the beer's flavour, even when having been subjected to a mysterious special process of 'beer sweetening.'

This left the field open for a variety of rigid but adjustable systems. Glass, and later the proprietary Pyrex, were common in the first part of the twentieth century but by mid-century the material recommended by the (then) Brewers' Society was stainless steel. All the rigid tube systems were similar, fixed beer mains to the bar pumps ran along the cellar ceiling with drop down swivel connectors to which a telescopic down pipe would be fitted. The bottom of the down pipe connected to the cask tap via a two-axis universal joint. The whole multitude of joints and telescoping tubes had sealing washers and tightening/clamping nuts. Cleaning involved rodding out the pipework with long brushes – a practice that is advised by some even now for plastic pipe, the brushes, three metres long, are still in equipment catalogues.

All this classic engineering was swept away within a few years by a simple plastic tube.

Check valves, non-return valves and bleed-off valves

THERE ARE A number of inexpensive gadgets that address specific cellar problems. Three such are these specialised types of valve.

There are occasions when it is desirable to be able to serve beer through a beer engine from a cask stillaged on the same level or even *above* the level of the engine. This is impossible with a normal handpump, since the valves in the cylinder and the piston have almost no resistance to pressure in the forward direction (only the weight of the valve); beer will flow continuously from the outlet. To overcome this problem a **check valve** must be introduced into the beer line.

The check valve is spring loaded, either adjustable or pre-set, and is regulated so that it will not open until the set pressure difference is established across it. This pressure difference has to be more than the maximum differential head of the beer (that is, the head between the top surface of the beer in the full cask and the pump outlet tap). It does open, however, when the pump is pulled, since this produces a suction, increasing the pressure across the valve. These valves can be fitted anywhere in the beer line between the cask and the engine. Some makes of beer engine can themselves be fitted internally with biasing springs on the cylinder inlet valves, achieving the same result. These are usually known as **high pressure engines**.

The **non-return valve** solves another problem: the worn pump. Pumps with worn or leaky inlet valves tend to run back if left unused for a few minutes; beer in the cylinder drains back into the cask. This causes great frustration, needing many pulls to get each pint. The run back also often disturbs the sediment giving rise to constant complaints of cloudy beer and by emptying the pump each time it also leads to excess fobbing on the next pint.

Although the pump can be serviced to repair the inlet valve it is often thought quicker and cheaper just to fit a non-return valve. The non-return valve is simply a replication of the inlet valve in the pump cylinder. It can be placed anywhere in the beer line but it is perhaps best fitted directly at the tap end. The advantage of this is that beer lines can be disconnected without any beer escaping. The simplest form is just a loose ball, which seats by gravity (if fitted at the loose end of the line connected to the cask, make sure that the pipe run keeps it roughly upright). As previously mentioned, a cask tap is available with its own non-return valve built in.

The **bleed-off valve** (also the **beer saver**) is a valve that is inserted into the beer line in the bar area near the dispense pump. Its purpose is to conserve the beer left in the lines at the end of any trading session. The device contains a fine, controlled needle valve which, when opened, admits air to the beer line; this allows the beer to run back into the cask at a slow, controlled rate. Such a trickle back avoids any disturbance of the sediment but still leaves the lines empty until the start of the next session. The habit to establish is to open the bleed at the call of 'time', then close it again perhaps 10 or 15 minutes later before quitting the bar. This leaves the line empty but sealed and ready to start the next session.

Most pump and cellar fitting manufacturers can supply a range of all these fittings to suit any size of beer line, although there might be problems if they are used with $\frac{1}{4}''$ (6.3mm) line and a gas assist pump system, as described in the next chapter.

Gas pumps (flojets)

In RECENT YEARS the simplicity of beer cask/plastic pipe/hand-pump has been, in thousands of outlets, complicated by the insertion in the beer line of another item, the gas powered diaphragm pump; now almost universally known by the trade name of one American brand, the **Flojet**. The reasons for their appearance in such large numbers are neither truly technical nor economic but rather a somewhat unexpected result of the general trend towards de-skilling cellar work.

The gas powered pump was introduced as a means of dispensing brewery-conditioned (keg) beers through free-flow counter units. It was a considerable advance on just relying on a top pressure of carbon dioxide or the better alternative of a gas mixture, since the partial pressures of the gases on the kegs could now be set with only the beer conditioning in mind. Most major breweries and pub companies fitted such pump dispense systems throughout their estates and it was here that the unexpected impact on handpumped ales occurred. The big companies' cellar fitting teams seemed to like standardisation and so Flojet pumps appeared in *every* beer line, cask and keg alike.

This is, of course, a generalisation, there are legitimate advantages to be had from using gas pump assistance in a handpumped system but nevertheless there remain many, many cases where it would be better to remove the added equipment and return to older, simpler ways.

The advantages that are to be gained are when the beer pipe run is either lengthy and/or has a large vertical drop. When driven by compressed gas at, say, three or four bar (50 psi) a Flojet has the potential to deliver beer into the line at a relatively high pressure.

Such a high pressure will overcome much line friction, so 1/4″ (6.3mm) bore tubing can be used and a vertical service of much more than a handpump's suction limit (which is the column of beer that can be supported by atmospheric pressure, in practical circumstances about eight metres) achieved. Using narrow tubing, again a standardisation move since both tubing and push-fit connectors are common to the keg services, means that line losses can be virtually ignored and problems of beer warming in the pipes much reduced. It is possible to install handpumped beer in bars several floors above a cellar – something that was only possible classically with complex linkages and remote pump cylinders.

However, because the Flojet, by its design, produces a high delivery pressure before cutting out, when used with normal handpumps that have no resistance to input pressure, beer would flow continuously. To prevent this, a check valve (see earlier chapter) must be fitted between the gas pump and the handpump, resulting in even more equipment that can be considered superfluous. In a normal pub set-up with the cellar beneath the bar and only a few metres of pipe run, gas pumps are totally unnecessary and, if presently fitted, their removal should be considered. They add the complications of much more hardware to maintain, a gas supply to pay for (even compressed air or extracted nitrogen is not free), more line joints to leak and more nooks and crannies where yeast can collect.

Beer temperature

CONTROLLING the temperature of the beer is a vitally important aspect of cellarmanship. The cellar should be maintained at 13°C at all times. In all but the most fortunate of circumstances, this means that a cellar cooler is essential and it may also, on occasion, mean that some winter heating is needed. It is a false economy to skimp on the cooler's power. If it has to run continually in the summer months, struggling to keep the temperature down, the bills for repair and early replacement will outweigh the extra cost of a bigger unit. To provide winter heat, an electric fan heater (wired in, no trailing leads on damp floors) or an extension from the building's central heating system is recommended. Never use any form of combustion heating in the cellar. A large, easy-to-read thermometer should be hung in the cellar, in a position away from draughts (particularly the air outflow from the cooler). Better still a remote reading unit, which nowadays cost just a few pounds, can be used with the readout in the bar area. This can add to customer interest.

The reason for setting such a precise temperature specification is, as has already been discussed in the chapter on carbon dioxide, the influence of temperature on the carbon dioxide content of the beer, its condition. As explained there, the amount of carbon dioxide that remains dissolved in the beer after venting, varies inversely with the temperature. Beer kept too cold will be over gassy and beer too warm will be flat. In-line coolers (flash coolers) should never be used for cask-conditioned beer, the cask itself must be kept at the right temperature. If an in-line cooler is used to try to correct a warm cask then flat, insipid beer will always result; if it is used to over-cool the beer then haziness is likely to occur.

Storage areas other than the cellar can present problems if they are uncontrolled. If at any time the temperature of beer gets down towards freezing point, it may develop a **chill haze**, which can be permanent. This haze is precipitated protein. This is the same precipitation that breweries induce when brewery-conditioned bright beer is chilled and filtered to remove proteins. A chill haze does not have much effect on the flavour of the beer but it will deter drinkers through its appearance. Of course, removing the protein by brewery conditioning does impair the flavour.

If beer is allowed to get hot, even for a short time, the result may be irreversible and disastrous. Above about 22–23°C finings undergo an irreversible change and lose all power to coagulate the sediment. Thus if a cask gets to such a temperature, even for a time too short for accelerated biological degradation to matter, there is a real danger that when cooled again it will never clear.

A further problem with temperature is rapid fluctuation. A cask that is settled and ready to serve can be made cloudy again by any sudden air temperature change causing convection currents to be set up in the beer near the sides of the cask, disturbing the sediment. Localised heat sources or cold draughts can have the same result.

The next section describes methods of cooling casks when an air-conditioned cellar is not available.

Cask cooling

As DISCUSSED EARLIER, the best way to keep traditional beer in its peak condition is to have an air-conditioned room, held at a constant temperature of 13°C. Happily, air-conditioning units are now quite affordable and virtually every pub has a temperature-controlled cellar. Yet there are still occasions – outside events for example – when other means must be found to keep the beer cool.

In former times the only solution was to use external **evaporative cooling**. Given sufficient attention this method can still prove extremely effective. The snag is that it requires constant work. The cask to be cooled is covered with an absorbent cloth: several layers of muslin cheesecloth or bath towels are good. Use natural cotton fibres that soak up and hold lots of water, synthetic materials are not so efficient at this. The cloth has to be kept permanently wet by frequent applications of water.

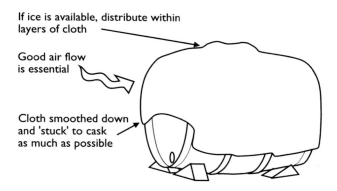

If ice is available, distribute within layers of cloth

Good air flow is essential

Cloth smoothed down and 'stuck' to cask as much as possible

Figure 27 **Evaporative cooling**

Temperature reduction is caused, not by the water itself (its original temperature is not at all significant) but by the evaporation of water extracting **latent heat** from the cask. For example, cold water at 10°C applied to a cask at 20°C can produce more than 50 times as much cooling from its evaporation as from its temperature difference. To get this sort of efficiency the evaporating water must be in close contact with the cask. The saturated cloth must stick to the cask surface as tightly as possible and the cloth should be fibrous to expose the maximum surface area to the air. There must also be a good current of air of low humidity to stimulate the evaporation and the cloth must be constantly damped down with a fine spray. In still, humid weather, evaporative cooling is not very effective. In this case the latent heat of melting can help somewhat. Crushed ice placed on the cask will also extract latent heat as it melts, however, a gram of ice melting into water only extracts about 15% of the heat that the gram of water would by evaporating. If plentiful ice is available and it is placed under and in the folds of the wet cloth, then the best of all results can be obtained; latent heat of both melting and evaporation is extracted and the supply of water to wet the cloth is extended.

If the beer is in an enclosed room (and without any electrical equipment) then keeping the floor constantly wet will help to reduce the room's air temperature by evaporation. Half a century ago this was standard practice in pub cellars.

Another external contact cooling method, not very cost effective and not recommended, is to use a plastic pocketed jacket (produced in roll form by one cellar equipment manufacturer). The pockets are filled with water and the whole put into a freezer – in effect it is a large version of the popular, flexible, ice cube sachet packs.

The first modern solution to the problem of cooling individual casks was to use IN-CASK COOLING PROBES. These are tubes that fit into the casks through their bung holes (where the shive is normally fitted). Cooled water is circulated through the probe and the beer can be kept at perfect cellar temperature even in a midsummer beer tent. The water flow must itself be cooled to remove the heat being withdrawn from the casks; it is normally supplied by an ice-bank re-circulating refrigerator unit. Cooling probes are very efficient but there are a number of drawbacks. The most obvious is the question of hygiene. As the probe sits in the beer throughout its service it must obviously be kept meticulously clean and sterilised between casks. To insert the probe the shive must be removed and then the cask is kept sealed by a rubber moulding at the top of the probe. This seal is not always perfect and there is a danger of beer losing condition. If the water circulated through the probe is too cold, close to freezing point, two problems resulting in cloudy beer can arise. Local chill haze can be produced in the beer around the probe and the large temperature differences can set up convection currents powerful enough to disturb the sediment (there has to be some convection, otherwise the bulk of the beer away from the probe would not be cooled).

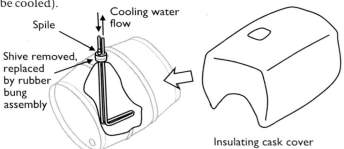

Figure 28 **In-cask cooling probe**

A way to avoid these problems that is now becoming the method of choice is to use WATER-COOLED CONTACT SADDLES combined with high-efficiency insulating jackets. The saddles are shaped from thin, stainless steel tubing as shown in figure 29, and clip onto the tops of the casks. Cooled water is circulated from a refrigeration unit as already described for the in-cask coolers. A cask is cooled partly by direct contact but much more by the intermediary of the air in the space between the cask and the insulating jacket being kept cold. Up to eight or ten casks are normally connected to a single cooling unit. Providing the jacket is kept well fitted, and preferably with some insulation under the cask as well, a differential of 12–15°C can readily be maintained between the beer temperature and the ambient air.

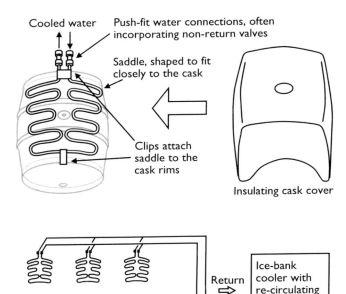

Cooled water

Push-fit water connections, often incorporating non-return valves

Saddle, shaped to fit closely to the cask

Clips attach saddle to the cask rims

Insulating cask cover

Ice-bank cooler with re-circulating pump

Return

Flow

Typical multi-cask cooling layout

Figure 29 **Cask cooling saddle**

A final method of cask cooling to mention is the use of localised air coolers. Commercial examples are available as completely self-contained units that will sit on a bar top to take just one cask, simply requiring connection to a power socket.

In considering questions of beer temperature one must appreciate the large thermal inertia of a full cask of beer. Whatever the temperature outside a cask, the beer inside will change its temperature by only a few degrees per hour. This can be the vital saving factor in what at first sight might seem hopeless conditions. Even on a hot summer's day, the heating during the open sessions can be partly offset by cooling the room as much as possible overnight. The beer temperature will then be closer to the average temperature of the room/tent integrated over the whole 24 hours.

Preparing racked beer

THE NORMAL RESPONSE of many licensees, when asked to provide beer for an outside function, is to offer keg beer only. If traditional beer is asked for, the answer is often: 'The premises are not available beforehand,' or 'it will be too warm to leave the beer to settle.' Yet beer was drunk at these events long before keg beer was invented, so why not now? The solution is simple: **racked beer**. With proper preparation, real ale takes no more effort to provide than keg, repaying the effort every time by its popularity.

The beer to be racked should be set up in the cellar, conditioned and tapped in the normal way; try to keep the condition on the high side. However, ensure that the tapped cask is several feet above the floor level. Take a newly-emptied cask and remove both keystone and shive, empty the lees and swill the cask out thoroughly with a cold water hose to remove all residual yeast and hops. It is not essential to make the cask sterile but you must use one that has only just been in use and has contained no sour beer. Drain the water and fit a new keystone. Check the beer in the set up cask and connect a short length of beer line to its tap. Insert this line into the empty cask right to the bottom and fill the cask.

It is important that the beer is transferred in this way, filling the new cask from below the beer surface, as this preserves the condition, prevents fobbing and minimises aeration. Keep a close watch on the beer flowing through the line to see that it remains clear; stop racking at the first sign of a thread of sediment being drawn off. The cask of racked beer should be filled completely and then have a new shive fitted. This is easy if the donor cask is a full kilderkin and the recipient a firkin but when they are the same size the last one or two pints may have to be made up with beer drawn from the normal handpump supply (no sparklers). Many licensees find that the five gallon polykegs, often used for cider, are very convenient for racked beer, although if you use ones that have actually been used for cider then a great deal of washing is needed. Any clean, used bag-in-a-box polypins are also worth retaining as being very useful for racking. Many breweries will provide racked beer on request, sometimes for a small premium per cask.

Do not tap or spile the cask until the moment it is needed for service. Bear in mind that the beer is now bright, so there is no longer any need to avoid moving the cask – it can be tipped up to the last drop. However, since the beer is bright, it will not maintain its condition for very long; any re-racked beer should be used within 24 hours, preferably less.

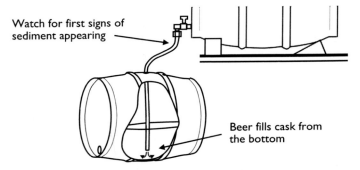

Watch for first signs of sediment appearing

Beer fills cask from the bottom

Figure 30 **Preparing re-racked beer**

Fining and re-fining

ISINGLASS FININGS, made from swim bladders of fish, and already mentioned in the chapter on conditioning, are most curious and mysterious. The substance is virtually pure collagen, a protein molecule with long intertwined coils and carrying a positive electrostatic charge. Yeast cells carry a negative charge, so when the finings are added to beer the initial clarifying action is electrical; the isinglass and yeast attract each other and flocculate into loose, fluffy lumps. The long, coiled collagen molecules also act physically as a sort of net, entrapping other protein materials into the coagulating sediment.

Fifty years ago, fining the casks in the pub cellar was part of the normal duties of a cellarman. Later, the breweries took over the task, sending the unfined beer out to a network of depots where the casks were left to condition for a week or two. The finings were then added just before delivery to nearby pubs. This was probably the optimum method for final beer quality but inevitably, cost-cutting set in and local depots have all but disappeared. The norm now is for the finings to be added to the casks in the brewery directly the beer is racked.

Nevertheless, occasions can still arise when it may be necessary to fine, or rather, re-fine a cask. Sometimes a cask gets missed or the fining station injects an inadequate amount. Also, if a cask has an interrupted journey (something all too common today) the finings will have settled the beer at each break only for it to be shaken up again on the next stage. This cask may well need re-fining since finings lose efficiency each time they are made to work, a state known as having **tired finings**.

If a cask has been vented, left to settle for a few days and it is no longer working vigorously, yet, when sampled, is still uniformly turbid, then it is unlikely to clear without some treatment. It could, of course, be one of the infections that beer is prone to, but smell and taste should make this obvious. Needless to say re-fining will do absolutely nothing for beer infected with wild yeast or bacteria. Should the sample show lumpy or fluffy clumps of sediment in a more or less clear liquid, then the chances are that the cask will clear eventually if left. It can, however, be quicker to add fresh finings and start again.

When a cask has to be fined, the procedure is simple. Firstly, take out the shive. A special de-shiving tool is available for this but a chisel or large screwdriver will do (be careful not to damage the wall of the bunghole in the cask). Pour off enough beer to make room for the required amount of finings and then pour in the finings. The finings must now be thoroughly mixed with the beer. The best method is to roll the cask about vigorously (drive in the new shive first!) but if there is no room for this the beer can be stirred with a clean, sterile rod inserted through the bunghole and rotated in a conical motion. Re-vent the cask immediately the procedure is complete.

The quantity of finings to use is proportional to cask size and, to some extent, is determined by the type of beer – more for the higher gravities. For most normal beers a fining rate of one pint per nine gallons should be adequate, rising to one and a half pints for a strong ale.

As has been mentioned, finings are destroyed by high temperatures, they should be kept in the cellar or in a cold store. Finings must also be fresh, once mixed they have a shelf life of just a few weeks. It is easy to see if finings have been damaged by heat: the liquid loses all its viscosity and becomes watery; in this case, throw it away.

Perhaps the most difficult part of the re-fining process is obtaining the finings in the first place. If you have friendly relations with a local brewery then a personal call will usually produce a couple of litres, *gratis*. The big national companies with their giant mechanised depots are not normally a fruitful source. Some pub chains have designated licensees who hold small stocks for emergency use. It is also possible to buy dried isinglass flakes, with a considerable shelf life, which can be made up into solution as required.

To assist the action of finings there are a number of proprietary tablets, powders and liquids that can be added. These are known variously as **finings accelerators**, **adjuncts** or **auxiliary finings**. There are many brands and they have a variety of actions. Some help to speed up initial fining and are added with the finings, others can be added on their own to revive tired finings. Many under the title of auxiliary finings also work by electrostatic action but have the opposite charge to the normal finings; these are added on their own. However if they do not succeed then any subsequent treatment with normal finings will need an extra dose since some will be used up neutralising this initial shot of auxiliary finings. Always consult and follow the makers' instructions.

There is a quick test that can be conducted to determine if a suspect cask will benefit from fining. Take a large, wide test tube, pour in a little finings, shake the tube and then pour out the surplus. This leaves a small quantity coating the inside of the tube. Fill the tube with some of the beer and shake it well. Hold the tube in the hand to warm it slightly and then watch the results. If the beer in the tube starts to clear in a minute or two, then the cask can be fined. If a test tube is not available, half pint straight or highball glasses will serve, it will just take a few minutes more. To try the effects of any of the proprietary additives, use a matrix of glasses with: no finings, primary only, primary plus auxiliary and auxiliary only, if necessary in various concentrations – comparing the results will soon show if there is any hope of resurrection. If all these tests fail, then the cask should be returned to the brewery for examination.

This test is instructive in demonstrating the complex action of finings. A demonstration is best done in something like a straight pint glass or beaker, using about a teaspoonful of finings. The whole process can be seen in half an hour or so. Initially there is flocculation into very loose, fluffy lumps, distributed throughout the beer. The smaller lumps amalgamate and eventually form into bands or layers, alternating with clear beer. The bands move through the beer, some to the top and (more) to the bottom, even seeming to pass through each other, finally forming the top break and the bottom break with the clear, fined beer in between.

One of the most mysterious and irritating, although rare, aspects, is the phenomenon of **layering**. On occasions, a cask of beer will be perfectly bright for the first few gallons and then suddenly cloudy beer will start to appear, without any disturbance to the cask whatsoever. This may continue for two or three pints before clear beer resumes. The explanation is in the action of the finings. On rare occasions, rather than all the sediment sinking to the bottom or rising to the top, a thin horizontal band or skein of sediment will stabilise at some position in the body of the beer. Such a layer, which can be very thin only affecting a few pints of beer, will not move if left. The only solution is to draw through it. Fortunately, this is quite an uncommon event and is never the first reason to look for if you have cloudy beer although most licensees will have experienced layered casks a few times.

HISTORICAL NOTE: *There are many folk recipes advanced for curing badly fined casks. One suggests pouring several kettles of boiling water over the outside of the cask, while another guarantees success by pouring a pint or more of soda water into the cask! In both instances there are probably germs of scientific truth lurking within – the hot water will set up convection currents from the base of the cask, up the walls and out onto the surface, these might raise some finings to have another try. The soda water, if poured carefully (perhaps via a tube or funnel?) could go into the cask bottoms where its effervescence will again rouse the finings. There are easier ways...*

Beer recycling

THIS IS AN EMOTIVE SUBJECT. There are a number of practices that fall within the description of recycling; the first is returning beer to a cask. **This is a bad practice at any time and cannot be recommended**.

In the past, it was without doubt the most common reason for traditional cask-conditioned beer getting a reputation for inconsistency and for being looked upon with grave suspicion. The days of one pump being kept for mixed drinks and serving strangers while a second with the 'same' beer was for the regulars in the know are long gone but unhappily filtering back does still go on, albeit in a more clandestine fashion. This is despite virtually all brewers publicly condemning the practice (but doing almost nothing to enforce such condemnation), despite the British Beer and Pub Association being on record as reproving the idea, and with little help from environmental health authorities who generally treat the matter with indifference. One of the main marketing reasons that brewers advanced for introducing keg beers was that they were tamper-proof (not, as it turned out, actually true) and so prevented the returning of beer. Perhaps the equipment manufacturers should bear much opprobrium as their catalogues are still replete with devices to achieve filtering back – there is even one (not listed in the appendix) that offers for sale a money spinning device that allows beer to be inserted into pressurised kegs!

For licensees who feel that there is still something to be gained, there are only two plausible cases when beer might be returned to a cask, although it has to be repeated that the quantities involved normally make it not worth the effort expended or the risks incurred. One is the case of the small quantity of beer recovered from a controlled venting spile, already quoted, the second is sound beer drawn off of lines prior to their cleaning. In this instance, co-ordinating cleaning with cask changes is a better solution and re-examining the line size and layout is recommended.

It is also worth examining the size of the lines in use. The plastic piping used for draught beer comes in three basic sizes: 5/8″, 1/2″ and 3/8″ internal diameter and if gas driven auxiliary pumps are in use then these are likely to be piped in 1/4″. It has been common in the past to use the larger size but this is very wasteful, holding much more beer per metre than the smaller bores; the lengths of piping per pint of beer are approximately:

5/8″ (15.9mm) bore	2.9 metres/pint
1/2″ (12.7mm) bore	4.5 metres/pint
3/8″ (9.5mm) bore	8.1 metres/pint
1/4″ (6.3mm) bore	18.2 metres/pint

Clearly, a typical pipe run of, for example, ten metres, would hold over three pints in the large 5/8″ bore but under one and a quarter pints in the 3/8″ pipe. Re-piping large bore systems in 1/2″ or if possible 3/8″ will pay for itself many times over in cost savings and quality improvements. The only drawback is a marginally heavier pull on the handpumps. Savings can also be found by routing the pipe work by the most direct path. A simple re-piping exercise often transforms the wastage equation so that returning beer becomes unworthy of any consideration.

At the risk of repetition, the sources of returned beer cited above are the only two acceptable. Even so the practice must be strongly discouraged and is generally a false economy when the decline of beer quality and hence the pub's reputation is considered.

In either case, the beer to be returned should be filtered into a sterile container and a sample must be tasted. If this test is satisfactory the beer should then be returned *immediately* via a sterile funnel. Alternatively, the sample can be tested first and the filtration then performed directly in the funnel (usually referred to as a **tun dish**). A new filter paper must be used every time. The cask should never be less than half full and the addition should never form more than a tenth of the cask's contents. It is worth noting that returning beer to any cask other than the one from which it originated is a criminal offence.

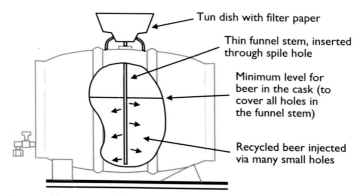

Tun dish with filter paper

Thin funnel stem, inserted through spile hole

Minimum level for beer in the cask (to cover all holes in the funnel stem)

Recycled beer injected via many small holes

Figure 31 **Using a tun dish filter funnel**

It is a common sight in many pubs, whenever a new cask is put on, to see one or two gallons drawn off from the pump for later (often much later) return to the cask. With proper attention to the casks in the cellar and to the cleanliness of the lines, this is never necessary. In particular, over-stooping can mean that sediment is drawn into the line from the old cask; as can repeated pulling of the pump to get the last few ounces of beer. Filling the lines with finings and dead yeast and then having to wash them out each time with fresh beer, is a regime of obvious absurdity. Another quite widespread practice, driven by avarice, is filtering back the bottoms of finished casks. How many licensees, indulging in this deceit, would drink a glass of what they are putting into their good beer? Any beer being returned should be good enough to sell over the bar in its own right. If not, then it is sharp practice, deceiving the customer with goods not of the quality demanded.

Categorically, the best plan is not to have a thin-stemmed funnel in the cellar at all but to concentrate on good beer management. Many polished copper tun dishes adorn the walls of pubs as curios of former times, we look forward to the day when they can be seen nowhere else and the stainless steel ones join them too.

The second broad class of recycling is immediately at the point of dispense, in England this is by means of **auto-bac** (also **auto-vac**, **auto-bak** and **economiser**) handpump and in Scotland with a **McGlashan beer recovering dispenser**. Again this subject raises strong emotions – many Yorkshire drinkers defend the auto-bac pump as the only possible way of ensuring the head on their pint as they like it. In both systems the principle is the same, overspill beer accumulates in the pump or font drip tray and the base of the tray is connected by a small pipe to an injector in the pump or font body. When a pint is served a small quantity of the overspill is sucked into the main flow by the injector operating on the Venturi principle (analogous to the way petrol is sucked into the inlet airstream going through the throat of an engine's carburettor). A small float valve shuts off the connection when the tray is empty, preventing air being sucked in.

These re-circulating dispense systems are now falling out of use although a few can still be found in the more traditional pubs of Leeds and West Yorkshire and in the bars of Glasgow. Their consignment to history, although it may be regretted by the nostalgic, cannot but be welcomed by most.

The third and last recycling system is so outrageous and such an example of sharp practice that it is amazing that supposedly legitimate businesses are allowed to sell the equipment and that Trading Standards authorities make no efforts to prosecute users. This is a device, made by a number of manufacturers, in a number of forms, but all of a basic style – the **beer conserver**. In essence this is just a vessel, the size of a large bucket, connected to a special valve in the beer line running from the cask to the pump. As each pint is pulled through the line a pre-set amount of the bucket's contents are mixed into the beer. The makers will explain that the bucket should be filled with good, recovered beer; it will not take the reader long to realise that the bucket can be filled with anything, starting with the cheapest, water. Should anyone have the misfortune to be employed in an establishment using such a device the advice must be first to seek an alternative appointment and then to give as much publicity as possible to the malpractice.

The head on a pint

ALTHOUGH ONLY PARTLY under a cellarman's control, the state of the head on a glass of beer and its desirability (or not) is a frequent topic for bar room discussion, often heated, frequently emotional. Some technical facts cannot go amiss.

Pour water into a glass – it does not form any head of froth. Even pulled through a handpump fitted with a tight sparkler it will not form a head. So head formation is not a property of water. Even with water heavily saturated with carbon dioxide (soda water, lemonade etc.) no lasting head is found other than the very transient bubbles released on pouring; so head forming is not a property of the carbon dioxide either.

The ability to produce a persisting head of foam is a property imparted to beer by another of its many minor constituents – a specific range of the proteins present. Within the bewildering array of organic chemicals in beer are some known as glycoproteins, which are responsible for this action. A glycoprotein is a large molecule with a protein head that is hydrophobic (water hating) and a long, hydrophilic (water loving) carbohydrate tail. Whenever a bubble is formed the hydrophobic heads of these molecules migrate to the bubble's surface (in effect trying to get out of solution) while the hydrophilic tails remain in the beer of the bubble's wall (trying to pull the molecule back into solution). The overall result is that the bubble acquires a 'skin', which greatly increases the viscosity and hence the stability of its structure.

This is not by any means the whole story. At least two other factors are vital, not only for the production of the head but also for its appearance, stability and effects on the beer's palate. First is the mechanism producing the bubbles and second is the gas within them.

With an ordinary short spout handpump or with gravity dispense, random sized bubbles are produced simply by the turbulent pouring of the beer; the result is the typical loose, Southern head of large, irregular bubbles containing mostly trapped air. There is no effect on the taste or mouth-feel of the bulk beer. If the handpump is fitted with a tight sparkler the beer is forced through a number of small orifices, which have two effects: the agitation causes carbon dioxide to break out of the beer (similar to the effect of shaking a can of beer before opening) and the small streams of beer will entrap more air in smaller, more uniform bubbles. The result is the classic Yorkshire head – a compact mass of small bubbles containing carbon dioxide as well as air. This style of head does have an effect on the bulk beer. Breaking out the carbon dioxide also brings out some of the aromatic hop oils giving an enhanced aroma to the pint although the beer below will be slightly less bitter and will have a little less condition than the same beer poured naturally. Aficionados will say that such beer 'drinks smoother.'

In recent years the **swan neck** has been widely introduced on handpumps. This long, vertical spout with a sparkler at the bottom reaches to the bottom of the glass and as the glass fills dispenses the beer from below the surface. At first sight this would seem unhelpful since there can be no entrapment of air, however another aspect of physics is at work – the Bernoulli principle, which to some is a quite counterintuitive notion.

With liquid flowing in a pipe in which there is an obstruction, to get past the obstruction the flow must speed up (liquid, being incompressible, flowing at a given volume per second has to go faster to get through a smaller area). To get this acceleration requires that the pressure must drop in the region of the obstruction; it is this pressure drop that makes the swan neck effective. As beer flows out through the sparkler the sudden pressure drop in the orifices breaks out dissolved gas, principally carbon dioxide. The many small bubbles produced at the bottom of the pint now rise through the beer eluting aroma compounds *en route* and giving the final tight style head. Again the bulk beer will be somewhat lower in condition and with enhanced (though perhaps more transient) aroma.

The production of creamy heads has been taken to extremes with keg stouts and keg 'smooth' bitters now served under top pressure of a nitrogen/carbon dioxide mixture. Although nitrogen is only one-sixtieth as soluble as carbon dioxide, enough does dissolve under the dispense pressures used to have a large effect. When the gas break out fills the bubbles with nitrogen they are much more long lasting – a bubble filled with carbon dioxide eventually collapses because the gas dissolves in the bubble wall and is lost but nitrogen does this much less readily. Another way of viewing this advantage of nitrogen is that the bubbles can be very much smaller for a given lifetime – there is a positive pressure inside the bubble that is inversely proportional to its diameter, very small bubbles have very high pressures and carbon dioxide would dissolve out almost instantly. The ultra-small bubbles of a Guinness head can only be produced with nitrogen.

None of the foregoing will help to resolve the arguments for or against sparklers, swan necks or tight and loose heads, they are matters of personal taste. However, it is important to give consideration to how a brewer intends his beer to be served – the use, for example, of swan necks for every beer sold without regard to these intentions is just poor management, as is a refusal to adjust a sparkler to accommodate a customer's wishes. The drinker should vote with his feet in these circumstances and find a more tolerant house.

The ideal cellar

Most of the supplies and equipment needed in the cellar have been mentioned on the previous pages. This section attempts to summarise these with a description of the ideal cellar.

The need for cleanliness has been stressed and cannot be over-stated. The cellar must be kept scrupulously clean at all times. It should be considered as part of the whole beer dispensing system. A cellar should never be allowed to become a storage area for junk. It should always be forbidden to pets and it must be a no-smoking area.

Walls and ceiling should be painted white with a fungicidal paint or emulsion. The ICI Dulux paint company produces a proprietary paint specifically for beer cellars. The floor, which is best made of smooth, high strength concrete, industrial quarry tiles or stone slabs, must have good falls to a drainage point. A conventional sand/cement screed over normal concrete is usually not successful as a cellar floor finish as it tends to be too soft, cracking and flaking under the battering from heavy casks. If a screed is used, an epoxy-based industrial type should be used. If the cellar is too low to connect directly to the drainage system, a sump with an automatic, float-operated pump is required. The sump should be kept sweet with frequent additions of lime chloride bleach.

Good lighting is important. Fluorescent tubes are best as they generate least heat, but they should be in waterproof, exterior grade fittings. Ventilation is also essential, but not to such an extent that there are any localised draughts. Cellars that are closed, air-conditioned rooms should have the doors left open from time to time to allow an air change.

A large, deep sink (a Belfast type) with hot and cold water is needed. The taps should be fitted to the wall well above the sink so that buckets can be filled easily. The cold tap should have a thread-ed hose connection, or there should be a separate hose tap. There should be a hose with a pistol-style head to enable the floor, dirty casks, etc. to be controllably washed down.

Beer lines should be long enough to reach all the cask positions without stretching tight yet not leaving a lot of dead pipe. Each pipe must be marked with a prominent, indestructible, label iden-tifying its associated beer engine and/or the beer type. The lines should be kept up off the floor and should be wiped frequently with a damp cloth. This way the outsides will stay clear longer, making it easier to inspect the inner cleanliness.

Some sort of shelving or storage bin system is needed to keep all the small, loose items segregated and ready-to-hand. Good stocks should be kept of:

- Hard and soft spiles

- Keystones and shives (of sizes used by the supplying breweries)

- Cork bungs (two sizes, inner and outer keystone diameters)

- Tap washers and hop filters

- Chocks

- Bleach and pipe cleaning fluid (in marked cupboard as per COSHH rules)

- Pipe clips (Jubilee clips), spare tails and burrs (with compatible threads)

- Sterilising solution (e.g. Sodium metabisulphite) stored properly.

If the keystones or shives are wooden, they must be kept per-fectly dry. If allowed to get damp they will swell out of shape and cannot be used. Spiles, cork bungs and cask closures are usually supplied free by brewers although recently they have become much more frugal with their largesse.

As well as consumable items there should be a good kit of hand tools, kept in the cellar and not allowed to 'wander' off for other uses. Essentials are:

- Large, accurate, wall thermometer. Cheap, accurate, electronic remote-reading thermometers are now available so the cellar temperature can be shown in the bar.

- Heavy wooden or composition mallets (two minimum)

- Medium and large screwdrivers and a pair of pliers

- Spanners (to fit tap valve nuts, pipe nuts, keg fittings etc.)

- Pincers and/or mole grips

- Spiling tools (two minimum, as previously described), the controlled venting type is recommended

- A de-shiving tool

- Dipstick(s) marked for all cask sizes and stillage methods in use

- Short length (1 metre) of beer line fitted with a nut and tail (if re-racking is practised)

- A few plain, straight sided glasses for taking samples

- Tap cleaning brushes

- Small scrubbing brush for cleaning shives and keystones

- Small, sharp, pointed knife

- Heavy duty stainless steel bucket(s) and a number of large plastic buckets

- Mop and bucket for floor cleaning

- Hand-towels, soap, drying cloths etc.

Given such a cellar, and enough customers, excellent beer should be assured and a great satisfaction obtained from the exercise of the craft of cellarmanship.

Appendix 1
Wooden casks

THE NEAREST most readers will come to a wooden cask is probably admiring the roses in a cut-down half cask at the pub door. At the time of writing only one brewery still uses wooden casks extensively (Samuel Smith of Tadcaster) and only a handful more have any even for occasional use. However, mainly for historical interest and completeness, the anatomy of a wooden cask is given here.

The cooper's trade is one of the oldest in the world; casks have been made in much the same way for a millennium. So it is hardly surprising that coopering has evolved its own language, yet some of these terms are still current having been carried over into the modern realm of the stainless steel cask – the projecting rim around the top and bottom heads is still the **chime** or **chimb** and the broadest central part is still the **bilge**.

Casks were, and are, always made from oak, the best being Russian oak a closer and straighter grained wood – less prone to warping – than home-grown English timber. Interestingly, the whisky trade, which still relies heavily on oak casks, seems to favour imports from the other direction, mostly using American oak. The key to a cask maker's art is fashioning the staves, a wonderful piece of three-dimensional geometry. Staves start off as flat planks, which are tapered to each end into a cigar shape, with the sides bevelled to lie on exactly the intended radius when set in a circle. A side-to-side rounding that will be part of the cask's circumference is added and V-grooves, that will receive the **heads** (ends), are cut in each end. Still straight lengthways, the staves needed for the cask are assembled around a head and held together with an iron hoop. A fire or a steam pot is put inside this loose assembly to heat and soften the timber and then the top ends are

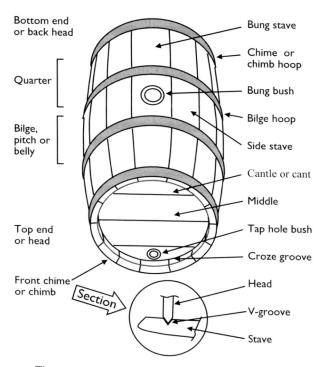

Bottom end or back head

Quarter

Bilge, pitch or belly

Top end or head

Front chime or chimb

Bung stave

Chime or chimb hoop

Bung bush

Bilge hoop

Side stave

Cantle or cant

Middle

Tap hole bush

Croze groove

Section

Head

V-groove

Stave

Figure 32 **The anatomy of a wooden cask**

drawn together onto the other head with a windlass – a sort of tourniquet – and the hoops are driven down to tighten everything up. The final shape of the cask is wholly determined by the profile of the tapers originally given to the staves.

Many believe that the classic bellied cask shape was evolved to make for better handling being easy to roll straight and yet turn at will, but this is just a happy serendipitous outcome of the production method. A cask can only hold together and be beer-tight if it increases in girth towards its centre, allowing the hoops to be driven tight by a wedge-like action. It would be impossible to make a cylindrical wooden cask.

The ends or heads, are made up from flat boards with chamfered v-shaped ends; they are doweled together to make the circu-

lar shape needed and again a wedge action is used to ensure tight-
ness – the chamfered edge is held wedged tightly into the grooves
in the staves by the tension in the hoop. A small amount of caulk-
ing compound may be spread in the groove first (historically, this
was often red lead paste!).

The front head boards always run horizontally, with respect to
the cask in stillaged position, the lowest board (a **cantle** piece) is bored
to take a brass or bronze bushing that will hold the keystone. The
rear head always had the boards running vertically. Another brass
bush was inserted into a hole bored in the top stave to form the
filling hole. The cast brass bushes (which were usually engraved with
the brewery's name and have since become collectors' items) have
a coarse thread on the outside and are screwed into the woodwork.

Although nostalgic minds often recall the pleasures of 'beer
from the wood' there were plenty of problems for both brewer
and publican. Despite appearing to be strongly constructed, oak
casks are surprisingly easy to damage – dropping a full cask just a
short way onto a concrete floor can crack a stave, dropping onto the
edge of the chime can burst open the head. In the brewery, cleaning to sterility is almost impossible and it was quite common for
casks to be condemned (to the rose tub market) after a persistent
infection had become established in the wood. In practice many
brewers did not actually allow beer to contact the raw oak at all,
their casks were lined throughout with pitch – their beers were
never 'from the wood' at all.

Of course one big advantage of the wooden cask is its low
thermal conductivity, it has its own built-in insulation jacket.
Provided a cask has been stored for many days in the cellar, it could
be placed on a bar counter for several days with the beer still stay-
ing at a tolerable temperature. This feature was so highly regarded
at one time by brewers that, with the advent of metal casks, several attempts were made to give them the same property. The Mills
cask was a more-or-less conventional stainless cask totally encased
in a wooden jacket (usually from moulded plywood), giving the
advantage of a decorative finish as well as the required insulation.
Another, decidedly non-decorative approach, was a double-skin-
ned steel cask with the space between filled with water; extremely

heavy and made even worse by having no appreciable chime to grip, they were not a success.

Leaks in wooden casks were fairly common and remedial measures could often be taken, with care, to cure some cases. The leak was almost always the result of careless handling, as mentioned, dropping a full cask was the usual cause. Small leaks will often seal themselves as the wood, freshly exposed to the escaping beer, swells up. If a cask was found to be weeping, it was vented at once to lower the internal pressure and then left for a few hours to see if it self-sealed. With a leak too large to leave, or one that did not seal, other steps were taken.

For a leak between staves in the side of the cask – (1) in figure 33 – then the nearest iron hoop could be tightened, driving it carefully a little further onto the curve of the cask. The ideal tool would be square-ended bar and of brass, to avoid cutting into the soft iron hoop.

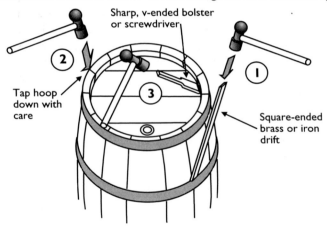

Figure 33 **Repairing leaks in a wooden cask**

For a leak around the edge of the cask end, tightening the end hoop (2) could be tried. Another unlikely sounding measure that could be surprisingly effective in this circumstance was to caulk the offending area (3) with hemp or even brown paper.

A leak between the end boards or a stave that is cracked across was not repairable *in situ*; it was a job for the brewery cooper.

Dipsticks

DIPSTICKS are essential cellar tools. They can be bought of course, or obtained from a supplying brewery but they are also easily made. For anyone wishing to make their own or to make any special combination of sizes, the following tables give some measurements. Use brass, aluminium or stainless steel rod about 6mm square. With square rod, four cask sizes can be engraved on the four sides. The approximate distances for the required markings (in millimetres from the bottom end) are given in the tables below for four cask sizes stillaged in the normal laid down mode, for two sizes in the upright, extractor dispense mode and, for completeness, measurements for a five gallon cider polycask (note that with polycasks, because they have re-entrant bases like wine bottles, a dip will show empty when there is still about half a gallon remaining).

In many instances – on double-height stillage for example – normal straight dipsticks are very awkward, a flexible one can be made from stainless strip (about 20–22 SWG). With strip, four sizes can still be accommodated by marking two from each end.

It goes without saying that dipsticks must be kept scrupulously clean and away from contamination (the author once visited a pub, that remains nameless and since then not revisited, where, through the open cellar door, the dipstick could be seen protruding from the floor drain it was being used to unblock…). A short piece of 22mm pipe with the end capped and fixed to the cellar wall makes a neat storage unit for several dipsticks.

Pin	Firkin	Kilderkin	Barrel	
Gls mm	Gls mm	Gls mm	Gls mm	Gls mm
1 86	1 69	1 57	1 45	19 300
2 137	2 116	2 84	2 68	20 312
3 185	3 140	3 110	3 86	21 324
4 243	4 170	4 133	4 104	22 337
4.5 291	5 204	5 155	5 120	23 348
	6 235	6 174	6 136	24 361
	7 266	7 194	7 149	25 373
	8 301	8 213	8 163	26 386
	9 355	9 233	9 177	27 399
		10 252	10 190	28 412
		11 271	11 202	29 425
		12 291	12 214	30 440
		13 311	13 227	31 455
		14 332	14 239	32 470
		15 355	15 251	33 487
		16 379	16 264	34 504
		17 407	17 276	35 525
		18 445	18 288	36 554

Measurements for normally stillaged casks

Firkin	Kilderkin		5 Gal. Polycask
Gls mm	Gls mm	Gls mm	Gls mm
1 50	1 40	10 282	0.5 5
2 96	2 72	11 307	1 34
3 134	3 102	12 333	1.5 65
4 171	4 129	13 359	2 93
5 209	5 155	14 386	2.5 122
6 246	6 181	15 413	3 152
7 284	7 207	16 443	3.5 180
8 330	8 232	17 475	4 208
9 380	9 257	18 515	4.5 240
			5 275

Measurements for casks on end

Figure 34 Dipstick dimension tables

Equipment suppliers

Angram Design Ltd.
Unit 11 Becklands Close, Roecliffe,
Boroughbridge, North Yorkshire YO51 9NR
Tel: 01423 324555   Fax: 01423 324955
Website: www.angramltd.com
e-mail: steve@angramltd.com

Beer engines both clip-on and cabinet styles of up to five pulls.
Quarter or half-pint cylinders, all available with water jacket cooling.

BevEx Ltd.
Telford Way, Stephenson Industrial Estate,
Coalville, Leicestershire LE67 3HE
Tel: 01530 834888   Fax: 08700 117 265
Website: www.bevex.co.uk
e-mail: admin@bevex.co.uk

All sizes of plastic beer line and fittings, including line in various
colours and made to order 'pythons.'

Easy-Rack
Dallas Street,
Mansfield,
Nottinghamshire NG18 5SZ
Tel: 01623 424242   Fax: 01623 661657
e-mail: easyrack@supanet.com

Individual auto-tilting frames.

England Worthside Ltd.

Hope Mills, South Street
Keighley, West Yorkshire BD21 1AG
Tel: 01535 682222   Fax: 01535 682223
Website: www.worthside.co.uk

*Supplier of beer engines in clamp-on and cabinet styles,
quarter and half pint cylinders*

Eurobung Ltd.

Roe Head Mill, Far Common Road,
Mirfield, West Yorkshire WF14 0DG
Tel: 01924 496671   Fax: 01924 480257
Website: www.eurobung.co.uk
e-mail: sales@eurobung.co.uk

*Plastic moulders of keystones, shives, spiles etc.,
also mallets and de-shivers.*

Filton Brewery Products Ltd.

The Coachmakers, 116a Seaside,
Eastbourne, East Sussex BN22 7QP
Tel: 01323 416948   Fax: 01323 431259
Website: www.filton.net
e-mail: sales@filton.net

*All types of cellar fittings and equipment including a wide range of
stillage systems. Originators of the external cask saddle cooling
system. A hire department provides package deals for temporary
events, beer festivals, etc. Comprehensive on-line catalogue and
ordering system on the website.*

Giles Enterprises

Corbin House, Gore Cross Business Park,
Bridport, Dorset DT6 3UX
Tel: 01308 459950   Fax: 01308 424410
Website: www.autoaletilt.com
e-mail: sales@autoaletilt.com

Racked, multilayer stillages and hoists, auto-tilt frames (including wheeled), cask cooling external saddles/jackets and automatic spile systems with built-in air filtration.

Gordon Dye and Son

3 Viking Court, Brompton,
Northallerton, North Yorkshire DL6 2DP
Tel/Fax: 01609 778437

Makers of the Race cask ventilator automatic spile.

Hallamshire Brewery Services Ltd.

Liverpool Street,
Sheffield, South Yorkshire S9 2PU
Tel: 0114 243 1721   Fax: 0114 256 0130
Website: www.hallamshire.co.uk

Cellar cooling systems and general beer dispense and cellar fittings

Harry Mason Ltd.

217 Thimble Mill Lane,
Birmingham B7 5HS
Tel: 0121 328 5900   Fax: 0121 327 7257
Website: www. harrymason.co.uk
e-mail: info@harrymason.co.uk

Old established supplier of all types of cellar/dispense equipment from washers up to complete stillage installations. The website has a comprehensive on-line catalogue.

Hi-gene Dispense Ltd. (subsiduary of Drinks Dispense Group)
Lakeside House, Turnoaks Park,
Burley Close, Chesterfield, Derbyshire S40 2UB
Tel: 01246 273166   Fax: 01246 271486
Website: www.hi-gene.co.uk *or* www.drinksdg.com
e-mail: enquiries@hi-gene.co.uk *or* enquiries@drinksdg.com

Handpump manufacturers offering both traditional and modern styles, including the Insight, which has a visible glass cylinder and dispensing tray on the bar top. Products include a huge range of continental-style pressure dispense fonts. The company runs a repair and refurbishment service for all makes of handpump

Homark Group Ltd.

Pottery Road, Parkstone, Poole, Dorset BH14 8RB
Tel: 01202 734000   Fax: 01202 737526

Beer engines in many varieties, half or quarter pint with insulation as required. Various check, non-return and aspirator valves, cooling cabinets. No website at the time of writing.

IMI Group plc.

Lakeside, Solihull Parkway,
Birmingham Business Park,
Birmingham B37 7XZ
Tel: 0121 717 3700
Website: www.imi.plc.uk

Huge conglomerate spawned from Britain's one time leading corporation, Imperial Chemical Industries (ICI). IMI grew by accreting companies in all sectors of engineering including many famous cellar/bar equipment makers and household name brands such as Gaskell and Chambers, Dalex and Optic. Until recently various group subsidiaries supplied a variety of cellar sundries and classical hand pumps but none of their very many websites now list any equipment for real ale dispense.

John Guest International Ltd.

Horton Road
West Drayton
Middlesex UB7 8JL
Tel: 01895 449233   Fax: 01895 420321
Website: www.johnguest.com

The leader in production of push-fit tubing connectors
of every description, with a vast on-line catalogue.

Kayel Engineering Ltd.
Elm Grove
Horsham, West Sussex RH13 5HX
Tel: 01403 261026   Fax: 01403 217340
Website: www.auto-tilt.co.uk
e-mail: info@auto-tilt.co.uk

Specialists in stillage systems, including self-tilting,
multilevel and units with full mechanical handling.

Murphy and Sons Ltd.
Alpine Street
Old Basford
Nottingham NG6 0HQ
Tel: 0115 978 5494
Website: www.murphyandson.co.uk
e-mail: info@murphyandson.co.uk

Manufacturers of primary and auxiliary finings.
Their website contains an excellent article on how
the different types of finings work.

Pennine Cellar Services
Units 7 and 8 Northend Road Industrial Estate,
Northend Road,
Stalybridge, Cheshire SK15 3AZ
Tel: 0161 304 8303   Fax: 0161 304 0217
Website: www.penninecellar.co.uk
e-mail: info@penninecellar.co.uk

Fairly new (established in 1994) general cellar equipment
supplier. Range includes metered pump, gas and electric pump
dispense, cellar cooling systems and general refrigeration.
Installation and servicing services in the North-west.

Rankin Brothers and Sons
Aylesbury, Bucks HP18 9BA
Tel: 01844 203100   Fax: 01844 203101
Website: www.rankincork.co.uk
e-mail: sales@rankincork.co.uk

*All forms of bungs, shives, spiles etc., also mallets,
de-shivers and many fancy wooden decorative items.*

Reunion Cellar Equipment Ltd.
The Speed Centre, Whitehouse Land,
Ivychurch, Kent TN29 0AL
Tel: 01797 366805   Fax: 01797 366905
Website: www.reunioncellar.co.uk
e-mail: widge@reunioncellar.co.uk

Suppliers of the Cask Widge flexible extractor system.

Tilt Master Ltd.
Mill Road
Barnstaple
Devon EX31 1JG
Tel: 01271 321232   Fax: 01271 344355

Auto-tilting stillage frames and stillage systems, hoists, etc.

Quick practical fault finder

The following section lists some problems that can arise with cask conditioned beer and gives suggestions for causes to investigate.

Cloudy beer from connecting a new cask:
- Beer is still 'working,' not yet dropped bright.
- Cask is infected (taste/smell will indicate).
- Beer has been disturbed in the cask; peg released too quickly; cask knocked; beer disturbed by filtering back.

(Testing the beer in the cellar before connecting the line would have found all of these problems.)

- Sediment in lines from the previous cask.
  Avoid attempting to pull the last few drops from a cask when the pump starts to draw air; do not over-tilt the casks.
- If using casks on end, with a rigid extractor.
  The extractor tube has been inserted too far down, into the cask sediment.

Cloudy beer suddenly, during dispense:
- End of the cask.
- The cask has been moved or disturbed; a self-tilting stillage has stuck and then released with a jerk.
  In these circumstances, stop dispense at once and investigate, the less yeast pulled into the lines the better. Flush lines out before reconnecting.
- Finings have 'layered.' This is very unusual, test for all other possibilities first.

Cloudy beer continually:
- Dirty beer lines or pumps.
- Leaky pumps 'running back.'
- Habitually filtering back poor beer.
- If frequent with finishing casks, over tilting of the cask.

Hazy beer:
- Lesser versions of any of the causes above.
- Beer has been allowed to get too cold, developing a chill haze.
- Finings may be 'tired' after too many cask movements.

Lumps and/or 'floaters' in the beer:
- Dirty pipes and pumps (with yeast lumps). Establish a regular cleaning schedule, once per week *minimum*.
- If debris is hop petals, hop filter missing or damaged.

Beer flat:
- Over venting, inadequate use of hard spile.
- Beer has been, or is, too warm.
- Poor glass washing.
- Beer too long in stock.
- Beer ruined by filtering back poor beer.

Beer too gassy:
- Insufficient venting.
- Beer has been conditioned at too low a temperature.
- In both cases allow more time for the beer to vent down to normal condition
- Some form of top/blanket pressure in use.

Beer has harsh, rough palate:
- Beer is 'green,' not long enough in cask to condition.

Beer sour, acetic:
- Infected, beer too long on dispense.
- Infected, filtering back old beer.
- Infected, beer too long in stock.

All above are beyond saving, return as ullage if possible otherwise destroy.

- A sudden acetic pint during dispense is the end of the cask. Stop dispense at once. Do not be tempted to think that as the previous pint(s) were received without complaint then the customer is mistaken.

Beer fobs on dispense:
- Air leak somewhere in the dispense system (may not show up as a beer leak, can be just 'one-way'). Gas powered pumps are especially sensitive to air leaks.
- Dirty pipes.
- Beer line has become kinked.

Pump will not pull full measure:
- Adjustable stop not set correctly for full stroke.

If adjustment of volume set-screw does not help, then check for: Leaky valve at pump cylinder inlet, leaking valve in the piston or wear in the pump barrel. If the situation always worsens after a few minutes without service and the pump requires several strokes to produce any beer then it is a leaking inlet valve, allowing beer to run back into the cask. Fit a non-return valve in the line (easy solution) or dismantle the pump and recondition the valve (harder solution).

Pump handle springs back:
- Cask tap not fully turned on.
- Cask still spiled or loose spile has been sucked back into spile hole.
- Beer pipe kinked.

Pump handle will not return:
- Piston valve is blocked or jammed (common if pumps are left out of use for a long period, especially dry).

Pump dribbles after use:
- Beer too lively, still working and releasing gas in the beer lines and pump barrel.

- Some parts of the beer lines run above the level of pump outlet. Fit a check valve in the line, re-route the line or add bias spring to pump inlet valve (only possible on some makes).

Keystones frequently split:

- The tap is not being held square to the keystone and in the centre of the cut-out.
- Excessive force with the mallet.

Glossary

Abv Alcohol by volume, now the official industry method of indicating a beer's alcoholic strength, always stated as a percentage. Almost all British draught beers tend to fall in the range of 3% to 9%.

Accelerators (to finings) Additives used to speed up the fining process. See chapter on Fining and Re-fining.

Acetic acid The chief chemical in vinegar. Beer, when infected with acetic bacteria, will turn to vinegar.

Adjuncts (in brewing) General term for various substances used by (some) brewers in smallish quantities either to impart specific characteristics to their beers (usually a laudable aim) or simply to economise on malt (usually at the expense of quality). The term is frequently used by beer drinkers in a pejorative sense as equivalent to *adulterants*.

Adjuncts (to finings) Various proprietary additives used to improve speed or efficiency of the fining process. See chapter on Fining and Re-fining.

Air filtration A practice occasionally used to prevent contaminants entering a cask. See chapter on Blanket Pressure.

Air pressure A traditional beer dispense method in Scotland. See named chapter.

Alcohol A saturated hydrocarbon in which one of the hydrogen atoms has been replaced by a hydroxyl (OH) group. The intoxicating chemical in all fermented drinks, C_2H_5OH, is ethyl alcohol, the second in the series – a waste product of yeast's metabolism.

Alcohol by volume See *abv* above.

Anker Archaic name for an archaic 10-gallon cask.

Aspirator Another name for a *demand valve,* see below.

Attenuation The degree to which a beer has had its initial carbohydrate fermented. A beer that is highly attenuated will be dry, without background sweetness.

Auto-bac See *economiser* below.

Auto-vac See *economiser* below.

Auxiliary finings Various commercial additives to help with clarifying a troublesome cask. See chapter on Fining and re-fining.

Barrel A 36-gallon cask. Not a general name for any other size of beer container.

Barrelage A method of measuring used in the licensed trade. A pub's annual wet sales are often quoted as the barrelage equivalent of so many 36-gallon casks. Brewery vessels also use the system; a 10-barrel plant can produce beer in batches of 360 gallons.

Beer conserver An outrageous device designed to make it easy for unscrupulous publicans to serve waste beer and to illegally water their beer. This work will not deign to describe its operation.

Beer saver See bleed-off valve, below.

Beerstone A dark brown to black mineral deposit resembling sand that sometimes appears from a cask. It is rare now with better cask washing, but totally harmless anyway.

Belly The curved, fattest part of a cask, also called the bilge.

Beer engine The classic mechanism for speedy and efficient service of cask-conditioned beer. A suction pump, usually mounted in or clamped onto the bar counter top. One stroke of the handle delivers either a quarter or a half pint, depending on the size of cylinder fitted.

Bilge See *belly* above.

Bine The climbing stems of the hop plant. Not *vine*, a common mistake.

Blanket pressure A discredited system for dispensing cask-conditioned ales. See named chapter.

Bleed-off valve A valve, fitted in a beer line near to the hand pump, that allows a small, controlled amount of air into the line. This breaks the pump's suction and allows the beer in the line to run back, under gravity, into the cask. They are used to empty the line during periods when there is no service (see chapter on valves). Also known as a *beer saver*.

Bottle-conditioned A bottled (as opposed to draught or cask) beer that has undergone a secondary fermentation within the bottle, frequently known as 'real ale in a bottle'.

Bottom break The band of yeasty sediment that falls to the bottom of the cask as a result of the action of the finings.

Bottoms The undrinkable sediment left in a cask after the potable beer has been sold, consisting of finings, dead yeast, hop debris mixed with a pint or so of beer.

Brewery-conditioned Beer that has been fully prepared at the brewery and usually filtered and kegged under pressure; also often pasteurised. Another name for keg beer.

Bright beer Usually used to refer to beer that has been filtered – in other words keg beer. However it is also sometimes used as a synonym for real ale that has been racked bright for quick set-up. *Racked beer* or *re-racked beer* are better expressions.

BSP British Standard Pipe, a system of thread sizes used in industry. The three-quarter inch size is becoming the common size for cask taps, beer lines, etc.

Bung The plug that seals a cask after it is filled at the brewery. Formerly a plain wooden disk driven into the bunghole (shive hole) and later replaced with a true shive after the beer was subsequently fined. Now, as beer is fined in the brewery on racking, the bung is the final shive.

Burr Another name for the nut that joins a beer line to a cask tap or beer engine.

Bush In wooden casks, brass or gunmetal rings screwed into the bung-holes and tapholes to receive the shives and keystones. Now, in metal casks, often used just to refer to these apertures. Also referred to as a *bushing*.

Butt A huge ancient cask of (usually) 108 gallons. Commonplace in Georgian times before the rise of industrial brewing, when beer was brewed in the pub and left for years to clarify and then served from the same vessel.

Cant The outermost boards in the end faces of a wooden cask (see appendix 1). Also known as a *cantle*.

Carageen Gelatinous alginate made from several varieties of red and brown seaweed added by the brewer as a clarifying agent during the copper boil of the wort before fermentation; also known as copper finings. More relevant to cellarmen, a component of some makes of proprietary *auxiliary finings*.

Caramel A burnt sugar, added to dark beers to give colour and its own style of sweetness. In recent years caramel has come under a slight cloud from vague claims that it may have some harmful properties.

Carbonation The addition of carbon dioxide to a liquid to produce a fizzy drink, usual for bottled beer, lemonade etc. A *carbonation unit* or *carbonator* automatically produces carbonated soda water for use with post-mix soft drink dispensers.

Carbon dioxide CO_2. Apart from alcohol, the main excreted digestion product of yeast. The presence of dissolved CO_2 in beer in the correct concentration is crucial to its flavour.

Cask The generic name for a container of cask-conditioned beer, real ale. Often used on its own to refer to the beer itself, as in 'mine's a pint of cask'.

Cask breather See *demand valve* below.

Cask-conditioned The descriptive name for beer that has undergone secondary fermentation, the essential requirement to be real ale.

Centres The central planks in the head of a wooden cask.

Check valve A spring-loaded valve that needs a set pressure difference before it will open. Used where beer may be stillaged above the level of a beer engine (see chapter on valves, also *high pressure engine*).

Chilled and filtered Description of brewery-prepared draught beer that has been cooled to a very low temperature to precipitate proteins and then micro-filtered to remove this precipitate and any yeast, etc. A dead keg beer that will then need carbonation and applied gas pressure to dispense.

Chill haze A fault with cask beer sometimes encountered if the beer has been allowed to become excessively cold. Some of the protein materials partially precipitate out as a colloidal milky haze. A chill haze does not usually have a serious impact on flavour as long as the beer is back at correct cellar temperature with correct condition, etc.

Chimb, **Chimbe**, **Chime** The projecting rim around the head of a cask; it rhymes with climb.

Chock A triangular wedge used in threes, to support a cask. See chapter on chocking.

Condition This normal English word has a specific, specialised meaning in the cellar world. It refers to the amount of carbon dioxide that is dissolved in beer, optimally just over one volume per volume. A beer with low condition will be flat and one that is over conditioned too fizzy.

Cone The flower head from the hop plant is usually known as the hop cone. The cone is also the basis of the valve in a traditional cask tap.

Copper A large brewery vessel, much like a gigantic kettle (a name also used, especially in the USA), to boil up the hops with the *wort* (q.v.). Traditionally made of copper, hence the name.

Crown cork The normal, modern seal for bottled beer, automatically crimped on in the bottling machine. Although cheap, easy to remove and seemingly completely liquid tight, it is not perfect, a crown corked bottle will not normally have as long a life as one with an old-fashioned cork.

Demand valve A device that allows a make-up gas to be admitted to a cask at exactly atmospheric pressure. See named chapter.

Dipstick A thin rod, marked with graduations, which can be inserted into a cask to gauge its contents.

Draught The word to describe a drink available in bulk form for dispense at the bar into measured units.

Drum A common name for a container of keg beer or lager.

Dry hopped/hopping See *hop* below.

Economiser A variety of handpump, gradually becoming obsolete, in which the overflow drip tray is connected to the pump cylinder so that overflow beer from one glass goes into the next.

Ethanol Another name for ethyl alcohol, the second in the series of so-called monohydric saturated alcohols, C_2H_5OH; the intoxicating element in all fermented drinks.

Evaporative cooling Cooling a cask by virtue of the extraction of the *latent heat* (q.v. below) needed to evaporate water from some cloth in contact with the cask.

Extractor A device that is inserted into the tap hole/keystone to enable beer to be drawn off with the cask stood on end. See chapter on such use.

Finings An extraordinary substance used for centuries to clarify cask beer. See named chapter.

Finishing gravity A measure (see *gravity* and *original gravity* below) of the density of the finished beer, gives some indication of the likely sweetness/dryness.

Firkin A 9-gallon cask. Probably now the most common size used for cask-conditioned beer.

Flash cooling Also in-line cooling – passing beer through refrigerated coils *en route* from the cellar to the dispense head. Normal practice for keg beer and lager, absolutely useless for cask-conditioned beer.

Flocculation The first part of the action of finings in clarifying beer. The yeast and undissolved protein particles clump together (by electrostatic forces, chiefly) into loose blobs or 'flocs.'

Flojet Trade name for one make of gas powered beer pump, now the generic name, see named chapter.

Fob Unwanted froth – frequently a sign, if dispense pumps constantly produce fob, of some cellar problem.

Free flow Usual name for the type of dispense font used for keg beers and lagers in which beer flows as long as the tap is held down.

Gallon Eight pints (4.546 litres). Despite metrication the gallon still dominates the brewing/pub industry as the day-to-day volume unit. Remember that the US gallon is only 80% of the Imperial gallon.

Gantry, gauntry Another name for a stillage to hold casks.

Gill A quarter of a pint, not a legal measure for sale of draught beer.

Government stamp The official mark engraved on a beer glass to guarantee its capacity is a true measure. It is illegal for a licensee to use any un-stamped glass for draught beer dispense other than through some special metering pump systems.

Gravity A word meaning density applied to brewing liquids from the wort to the final beer. *Original gravity* is described below *finishing gravity* above.

Green beer Beer that has not been adequately matured and conditioned, characterised by a certain roughness of palate.

Gyle (number) The brewer's way of identifying a particular brew batch, often marked on the cask but usually then not translatable by the customer into useful information.

Handpull The handpump or *beer engine,* see above.

Handpump The more common name for the *beer engine*, see above.

Haze Slight opacity in the appearance of a draught beer, usually only a cosmetic fault but can be serious if caused by infection. See *polish* below.

Head The circular, flat end face of a cask. The front head contains the tap hole and its keystone. The froth on the top of a glass of beer.

Headspace Empty space above the beer in a full cask. Casks are not units of measurement and are normally made slightly over their nominal size.

High pressure engine A hand pump that has a spring-loaded inlet valve. This requires a (pre-set) level of suction before the valve will open to admit beer. They are used where beer is stillaged on or above the level of the pump and could otherwise run straight through the pump.

Hogshead A 54-gallon cask, the largest size now in use anywhere but now very unlikely to be encountered by any reader of this edition of *Cellarmanship*.

Hoop One of the iron bands around a wooden cask to retain the staves in place.

Hop A vigorous climbing plant with aromatic flowers. The harvested flower spikes are dried and added, either whole or in a variety of processed forms, to the copper boil in the brewery. The flowers contain a complex mixture of resins and oils that give bittering and astringent flavours and aromas to the beer. Some varieties also give citric flavours, some have herbal tones. A number of brewers add a quantity of whole hops to each cask as it is filled (dry hopping); these add aroma and to some extent, by floating on the beer surface, act as a preservative.

Hop filter A small gauze strainer (looking very like a tea strainer from a dolls' house), inserted in the beer line between the cask tap and the dispense pump to catch any pieces of hop petal present in the beer.

Hopped wort Brewery language for the liquid that results from boiling the sugary liquid that was drawn off of the malt in the mash tun with hops. Yeast is added (*pitched*) to this hopped wort to start the fermentation into beer.

Horsing See *stillage* below.

Irish Moss Another name for *carageen*, see above.

Isinglass The correct name for *finings*, see above.

Keg General name for a container for brewery-conditioned beer (normally of a cylindrical shape rather than the bellied cask shape). By extension, has become the general name for the beer itself, as in 'mine's a pint of keg...'

Keystone The bung that closes the tap hole in the head of a cask, formerly always wood, now more frequently plastic. The tap is driven through the centre of the keystone to prepare the beer for service.

Kilderkin An 18-gallon cask. Now the larger of the two sizes (9 and 18 gallons) in common use. Frequently referred to as a kil or a kiln.

Lacing The appearance of a glass of beer served with a tight head in which the head, persisting throughout the drink, leaves visible rings down the inside of the glass. Considered by many as the sign of quality beer.

Latent heat Ice melts at 0°C and the water then boils at 100°C. But after a block of ice has melted, the water is still at 0°C, and after this has boiled the steam is still at only 100°C; although heat has had to be continuously put in to produce the melting or boiling yet the temperature has not changed. This is because to produce a change of state (solid to liquid, liquid to gas) the molecules must be given extra energy to 'break free' of their more constrained state. The energy needed to do this is the *latent heat of fusion* or the *latent heat of vaporisation* and it is very considerable. To melt a gram of ice requires the amount of heat that would heat the gram of water by 80°C and to evaporate it heat that would (if it could) raise it by 540°C! Nature understands latent heat, it is why evaporating sweat cools us down. Conversely, it is why a little steam from a kettle, condensing on a finger, burns more than the equivalent drop of boiling water – it has to give up its latent heat to condense.

Layering A rare fault in the fining process where a thin, stable layer of sediment forms in an otherwise clear cask of beer. The result is the sudden, unexpected appearance of cloudy beer for just a few pints.

Lees Another name for the yeasty sediment left in an empty cask.

Liquor Simply put, water. More precisely, in the brewer's vocabulary, the water that will eventually become beer (as opposed to any other water used simply for washing or cooling etc.).

Loose head The froth on the top of a glass of beer as it appears when served straight from a cask into the glass – a combination of random sized bubbles that start to collapse straight away. Many drinkers prefer their beer served this way. Compare with *tight head* and see The head on a pint chapter.

Mash the brewer's word for the process of steeping malt in hot water (*liquor*) to extract the fermentable sugars. An early step in producing beer.

Mash tun The large brewery vessel, often of many thousands of gallons capacity, in which the *mash* takes place. The inner base has a sieve-like structure to retain the malt (now known, after use, as *spent grains*) and allow the sugary water (*wort*) to be drained off.

Maturation The whole process of bringing cask beer to its perfect state before service but in general the word is normally used specifically to cover the need to keep the beer for a duration, often many weeks for a strong ale, prior to venting etc.

McGlashen tall font A handsome counter mounted dispensing head, formerly common in the many Scottish city bars that used an air pressure system of dispense. Usually incorporated a system to recover and recycle overspill beer. See chapters on Air pressure and Beer recycling.

Methanol Methyl alcohol (C_3OH), the simplest of all alcohols. Poisonous but also giving an initial intoxicating effect similar to ethanol.

Mixed gas A carbon dioxide and nitrogen mixture, the modern supernatant gas for keg beer, lager and stout dispense; pioneered by the Guinness brewery. See named chapter.

Molecular sieve A solid, often in the form of a thin sheet, whose molecular structure is such that that it is porous to some gases or liquids and not others. Design of such 'clever' materials is a major field of chemical engineering. In the cellar context the material of interest comes in units that extract nitrogen from the air – to a remarkable degree of purity, 99% or more. See chapter on Mixed gas.

Nip One third of a pint, the smallest legal volume of draught beer to sell (in a Government stamped glass marked at one-third pint).

Non-return valve A simple one-way valve that can be fitted anywhere in a beer line to duplicate the action of the handpump's inlet valve, usually as an easy repair for a worn handpump (see chapter on valves).

Original gravity A measure of the density of the wort before fermentation. It is quoted as a four digit number, roughly in the range of 1030 to 1100, the larger the number the more fermentable sugar present, hence the stronger the resulting beer. It is 1000 times the specific gravity, hence water (specific gravity 1) would be 1000. There is no direct translation into alcohol abv (see above) since in each case it depends how much sugar/carbohydrate is left when fermentation is complete (see *finishing gravity* above). A formula that works reasonably for most normal bitter beers is to subtract 1008 and then the divide the result by 8 – thus a 1045 OG bitter would be: (1043–1008) ÷ 8, i.e. 4.375% abv.

Partial pressure Simplistically, the molecules in a gas can be thought of as billions of tiny balls hurtling about at enormous speeds in totally random directions, constantly colliding with each other and with the walls of the container. It is this rain of molecules, rebounding from the container walls, that gives rise to the gas's pressure. In a gas, such as air, which is a mixture of several others, the incessant collisions share out the kinetic energy of all the molecules so that *on average* they are all the same. In this circumstance each gas is responsible for a share of the overall pressure in proportion to its percentage in the mixture. This is the *partial pressure* exerted by that particular gas in the mixture.

Pasteurisation Heat treatment in the brewery to sterilise beer before kegging or bottling (or, often for bottles, treatment of the whole filled bottle). Has a detrimental affect on the flavour.

Piggin A name occasionally used for a 2-gallon container of the bag-in-a-box variety.

Pin A cask of 4½-gallon capacity, now rare but possibly making a modest comeback.

Pint Despite the EU's, and hence Britain's, espousal of the metric system, our pubs and beer industry still use the Imperial pint as the basis for all draught beer sales. In fact, not only has the UK a derogation to allow this specific use of a non-metric unit but weights and measures legislation *insists* upon it. The only legal measures for the sale of draught beer are a third, a half and a full pint and multiples of a pint.

Pitch Another name for the cask *bilge* or *belly* (see above).

Pitching Adding the initial quantity of yeast into a vessel full of *hopped wort* to start its fermentation into beer. In traditional practice just throwing in a bucket of yeast scooped off of another fermenter, now a rather more scientific procedure!

Polish The top visual appearance of a glass of beer – crystal clear with a gem-like clarity. Not, however, a guarantee of flavour, an old acetic beer can frequently look more polished than it was when in drinkable condition.

Polycask A rigid plastic, cask-shaped container of 5-gallon capacity. A tap towards the bottom of the side allows the contents to be dispensed when the cask is stood upright. Normally used for draught cider or scrumpy, but can be useful for racked beer.

Polypin A flexible plastic bag with an integral tap, held in a cubical cardboard container. Usually holds about five gallons of beer, although smaller sizes are available.

Post-mix A system of soft drink dispensing that mixes various concentrated, flavoured syrups with centrally generated soda water in a flexible dispensing gun. (As opposed to pre-mix where the products are dispensed to the gun or fonts from containers already at the required concentration).

Primary fermentation The fermentation in the brewery, lasting about a week that all beer is subject to.

Priming sugar A sweet syrup sometimes added to beer at the brewery racking stage to stimulate subsequent *secondary fermentation*.

Puncheon An archaic cask of 72-gallon capacity.

Python A thermally insulating tube taking beer lines from the cellar to the bar. Cooled water is circulated through other pipes in the python to keep the overall temperature at the desired level.

Quart Two Imperial pints, a legal measure for serving draught beer.

Quarter Part of the body of a cask, see the appendix 1.

Race ventilator Trade name for one particular make of automatic cask spile, see the chapter on automatic spiles.

Rack To run beer off from one cask into another container to achieve beer without sediment for moving to a location for immediate sale. See Preparing racked beer chapter.

Racking tap A cask tap with a downwaed facing spout, meant for direct service from cask to glass. Sometimes knowb as a *turndown tap*; see chapter on Taps.

Ready-racked Another expression for beer that has been drawn off for instant use (see *Rack* above). Many breweries and beer wholesalers will provide such beer for a small premium.

Rolling hoops (rings) The two raised circumferential rings around a cask that help it roll in a straight(ish) line. In the brewery these often engage with a railway-like system to aid automatic handling.

Rope A bacterial infection (Zymomonas) that can ruin beer in a matter of hours, producing glutinous threads in the beer with an awful stench (hydrogen sulphide) and taste. So common in previous centuries that it gave rise to the common expression 'ropey' for anything of poor quality.

Scotch An old name sometimes used for a cask chock.

Secondary fermentation The essential process that is needed to produce real ale. A slow fermentation that takes place in the cask after it has been filled with (unfiltered) beer. Over a week or two it uses up residual sugars and, due to the reduced rate and the alcohol content of the beer substrate, it produces a differing mix of flavour compounds to those produced in the primary, brewery, fermentation. In essence, the yeast involved is living under stressed conditions and hence produces subtly different waste products.

Sediment The yeast, hop debris, finings etc. that lie in the bottom of a cask that has settled, ready for service.

Shive A wooden or plastic bung to stop up the cask's filling hole. A central depression or plug (the tut) is subsequently punched through to vent the cask.

Spigot A tapered, hollow plug that is inserted into the cask spile hole to allow connection to a make-up gas supply (e.g. from a *demand valve* see above).

Sparkler A small device screwed (sometimes integral) to the end of a dispense tap or spout. Designs vary, but essentially a series of restrictive orifices cause dissolved gas to break out of the liquid being dispensed to enhance the head on the beer.

Spile The peg, usually wooden, that is inserted into the spile hole in the shive after a cask is vented. While the cask is still evolving gas a porous, soft spile is used, then replaced with an impervious hard spile (wood or plastic).

Stave One of the curved planks forming the body of a wooden cask, see appendix 1.

Stillage A framework or a brick/masonry construction to accept casks to be prepared for service. To set a cask up into place is to stillage the cask.

Stooping Tilting the cask, see named chapter.

Strig A woody piece of the stem at the base of the hop flower that sometimes appears as debris in a beer line or filter.

Swan neck A long downward extension on the outlet spout of a beer engine, intended to reach to the bottom of the glass during filling. The outlet is fitted with a sparkler. See The head on a pint chapter.

Syphon See *extractor*, above.

Tail The combination of nut (burr), washer/hop filter and spigot forming the termination to a beer line.

Tall font An elegant brass or chrome pillar tap dispense head, traditional in Scotland. The tall font is an integral part of that nation's air pressure dispensing system and usually incorporates a special injector valve to recycle overflow beer. See chapter on Beer recycling.

Tap hole The aperture and bushing in the head of a cask that is stopped up with the *keystone* (see above) and eventually receives the tap.

Thrawls Another, less common, name for the *stillage* (see above).

Tight head A creamy head on a glass of beer, made up from very small, uniform bubbles and intended to persist throughout the drinking of the beer. Strong regional preferences both for and against exist. See The head on a pint chapter.

Top break A small amount of sediment that rises to the surface of the beer as a result of the action of the finings, responsible for that cloudy last pint from a near-empty cask. See also *bottom break,* above.

Top pressure A method of dispensing brewery-conditioned beers by applied gas pressure, anathema to real ale. See named chapter.

Tub Another common name for the container used for keg beer and lager.

Tun dish A large stainless steel or copper funnel with a very narrow neck able to fit into the spile hole of a cask, enabling otherwise waste beer to be recycled, see chapter on Beer Recycling.

Tut The central depression or plug in a *shive* (see above) through which the venting tool is driven and then the spile inserted.

Ullage Waste beer such as beer left in the bottom of the cask, spillage at dispense, beer drawn off for pump cleaning, etc. Most brewers have an ullage allowance although this is often parsimonious. Historically, ullage meant the volume by which a cask or vessel was under-filled but this usage has fallen out of fashion.

Vent To release the build up of carbon dioxide gas in a cask resulting from secondary fermentation (see above). See the chapter on spiling.

Volumes per volume A key concept in describing how a gas dissolves in a liquid. Because, at the atomic level, any substance is mostly empty space the molecules of a gas, say, can be accommodated amongst those of a liquid without requiring the liquid to take up any more space (i.e. volume). The extent to which this happens depends on several factors – the temperature, the gas pressure and the chemical properties of the substances – and, for any specific set of these, the volume of gas that a given volume of liquid can 'soak up' is fixed.

Water engine An unlikely device, common in Scotland during the nineteenth and much of the twentieth centuries to generate pressurised air for their traditional air pressure dispense system. See the Air pressure chapter.

Wet rent The traditional system for leasing a pub to a tenant by a surcharge on all the drinks supplied from the tying brewery. Now largely given way to more conventional property leasing agreements.

Wet trade The volume of drink sales in a pub.

Wort Brewer's language for the sugary liquid that has been run off from the malt in the mash tun. More exactly this is the *sweet wort*, in the next process it is boiled with hops to become *hopped wort*.

Yeast Microscopic, single-celled plant that metabolises sugary carbo-
hydrates and produces alcohol and carbon dioxide as its main waste
products. There are many varieties but for production of British style
ale and beer they all belong to the family *Saccharomyces cerevisiae*.
A yeast content of a million cells or more per millilitre of beer is
considered necessary for successful *secondary fermentation*.

Yeast count The number of yeast cells in a given sample of beer, usually
expressed in millions of cells per millilitre.

**CAMPAIGN
FOR
REAL ALE**

IT TAKES ALL SORTS TO CAMPAIGN FOR REAL ALE

CAMRA, the Campaign for Real Ale, is an independent not-for-profit, volunteer-led consumer group. We actively campaign for full pints and more flexible licensing hours, as well as protecting the 'local' pub and lobbying government to champion pub-goers' rights.

CAMRA has 75,000 members from all ages and backgrounds, brought together by a common belief in the issues that CAMRA deals with and their love of good quality British beer. For just £18 a year, that's less than a pint a month, you can join CAMRA and enjoy the following benefits:

- A monthly colour newspaper informing you about beer and pub news and detailing events and beer festivals around the country.

- Free or reduced entry to over 140 national, regional and local beer festivals.

- Money off many of our publications including the Good Beer Guide and the Good Bottled Beer Guide.

- Access to a members-only section of our national website, **www.camra.org.uk** which gives up-to-the-minute news stories and includes a special offer section with regular features saving money on beer and trips away.

- The opportunity to campaign to save pubs under threat of closure, for pubs to be open when people want to drink and a reduction in beer duty that will help Britain's brewing industry survive.

- Log onto **www.camra.org.uk** for CAMRA membership information.

DO YOU FEEL PASSIONATELY ABOUT YOUR PINT? THEN WHY NOT JOIN CAMRA

Just fill in the application form (or a photocopy of it) and the Direct Debit form on the next page to receive three months' membership FREE! If you wish to join but do not want to pay by Direct Debit, please fill in the application form below and send a cheque, payable to CAMRA, to CAMRA, 230 Hatfield Road, St Albans, Hertfordshire AL1 4LW.

Please tick appropriate box

☐ Single Membership (UK & EU) £18

☐ For under-26 Membership £10

☐ For 60 and over Membership £10

For partners' joint membership add £3 (for concessionary rates both members must be eligible for the membership rate). Life membership information is available on request.

If you join by Direct Debit you will receive three months' membership extra, free!

Title _____ Surname _____

Forename(s) _____

Address _____

_____

_____ Post Code_____

Date of Birth _____ E-mail address _____

Signature _____

Partner's details if required

Title _____ Surname _____

Forename(s) _____

Date of Birth _____ E-mail address _____

Please tick here ☐ if you would like to receive occasional e-mails from CAMRA (at no point will your details be released to a third party).

Find out more about CAMRA *at* **www.camra.org.uk**
Telephone 01727 867201

Instruction to your Bank or Building Society to pay by Direct Debit

DIRECT Debit

Please fill in the form and send to: **Campaign for Real Ale Ltd, 230 Hatfield Road, St. Albans, Herts, AL1 4LW**

Name and full postal address of your Bank or Building Society

To The Manager   Bank or Building Society

Address

Postcode

Name (s) of Account Holder (s)

Bank or Building Society account number

Branch Sort Code

Reference Number

Banks and Building Societies may not accept Direct Debit Instructions for some types of account

---

Originator's Identification Number

9	2	6	1	2	9

FOR CAMRA OFFICIAL USE ONLY
This is not part of the instruction to your Bank or Building Society

Membership Number

Name

Postcode

Instruction to your Bank or Building Society

Please pay CAMRA Direct Debits from the account detailed on this Instruction subject to the safeguards assured by the Direct Debit Guarantee. I understand that this instruction may remain with CAMRA and, if so, will be passed electronically to my Bank/Building Society

Signature(s)

Date

DIRECT Debit

This Guarantee should be detached and retained by the payer.

The Direct Debit Guarantee

■ This Guarantee is offered by all Banks and Building Societies that take part in the Direct Debit Scheme. The efficiency and security of the Scheme is monitored and protected by your own Bank or Building Society.

■ If the amounts to be paid or the payment dates change CAMRA will notify you 7 working days in advance of your account being debited or as otherwise agreed.

■ If an error is made by CAMRA or your Bank or Building Society, you are guaranteed a full and immediate refund from your branch of the amount paid.

■ You can cancel a Direct Debit at any time by writing to your Bank or Building Society. Please also send a copy of your letter to us.

detached and retained this section

BOOKS FOR BEER LOVERS

CAMRA Books, the publishing arm of the Campaign for Real Ale,
is the leading publisher of books on beer and pubs. Key titles include:

Good Beer Guide 2005
Editor: **ROGER PROTZ**

The Good Beer Guide is the only guide you will need to find the right pint,
in the right place, every time: the original and the best independent guide
to around 4,500 pubs throughout the UK, rated by The Sun newspaper in
the top 20 books of all time! Now in its 33rd year, this annual publication is
a comprehensive and informative guide to the best real ale pubs in the UK,
researched and written exclusively by CAMRA members.

£13.99   ISBN 1 85249 196 5

The Book of Beer Knowledge
JEFF EVANS

A unique collection of entertaining trivia and essential wisdom, this is the
perfect gift for beer lovers everywhere. More than 200 entries cover
everything from the fictional 'celebrity landlords' of soap pubs to the harsh
facts detailing the world's biggest brewers; from bizarre beer names to the
serious subject of fermentation.

£9.99   ISBN 1 85249 198 1

Good Bottled Beer Guide
Editor: **JEFF EVANS**

Now in its fifth edition, the Good Bottled Beer Guide is the bible for all
aficionados of bottle-conditioned beer. It is a comprehensive guide to the
huge number of beers now available in supermarkets, off-licences and via
the internet in the UK.
    Profiles of more than 600 bottle-conditioned beers, including bitters,
lagers, milds, wheat beers, stouts, porters, fruit beers and barley wines.

£9.99   ISBN 1 85249 197 3

Order these and other CAMRA books online at **www.camra.org.uk**
(overseas orders also taken), ask at your local bookstore, or contact:
CAMRA, 230 Hatfield Road, St Albans, AL1 4LW.   *Telephone* 01727 867201